Aleene

A "Tacky" Lady

by Aleene Jackson

ACKNOWLEDGEMENTS

I would like to thank my entire family, "and there are many of them", children, parents, aunts, uncles, cousins for helping me to create a fun and profitable life.

Also a real thank you to my customers, business associates, suppliers who through the years have "worked with me". Without them I wouldn't be having a "story to tell".

And finally, I'd like to thank my friend and editor, Steve Diamond, for his assistance in arranging the material of this book. To my son Fred Hershman who helped me choose from 1000's of photographs. A special thanks also to my grandson, Woody Hall for his assistance in laying out this book, and last but not least to Colleen McIlroy who was responsible for the final proof.

For information, address:
ENEELA Publications
85 Industrial Way
Buellton, CA 93427

copyright 1997

ISBN # 0-9656271-0-1

Table of Contents

Front row: Heidi Borchers, Tiffany Windsor, Candy Liccione **Middle row:** Tony Hershman, Aleene, Woody Hershman **Back row:** Fred Hershman.

Aleene's has truly been a family business. Not always perfect but always something special.

"Chapter 11"

You might think it's a bit curious to begin a book with the title "Chapter 11," but I promise you, it's not a mistake or a typo. I just felt that Chapter 11, which in the business world means *bankruptcy*, would be a good place to start a book about success.

In a recent magazine article, they called me "The Poor Woman's Martha Stewart," and compared our different approaches. I guess I'm rather proud of that label, because I've always tried to make our crafts accessible to everyone, starting from our earliest days of teaching "junk crafts," using common, everyday items found in the home.

Over the years, people have given me so much credit for success-- as one of the pioneers, I promoted the crafts industry in its earliest days, before it was the billion-dollar-a-year business it is now. I've started several businesses, created numerous crafts-related products, invented processes, taught classes, and wrote over 300 softbound books on "how-to" for everything from flower arranging to gold leafing, paper mache, special occasion decor, youth project designs, and all kinds of crafts-- but many things happened to me along the way to my success, and I want you to know about them.

Before there was a crafts industry, I had to write the books and the instruction sheets, go around the country lecturing and teaching crafts, appear on television in its earliest days, attend fairs and floral and home shows. Back when I started, the supplies, the materials and tools of the craft trade weren't even available to the public. It's sort of like movie stars who work for years and years, then when they get a hit show they're suddenly discovered, or labeled an "overnight success." The truth is, of course, they've been working hard at it for many, many years.

Some of you will know me from my products, the

most popular being Aleene's Tacky Glue, or perhaps from our successful television show "Aleene's Creative Living," hosted by my daughter Tiffany Windsor on The Nashville Network (TNN), or our monthly magazine, Aleene's Creative Living. But I know most of you don't know about the many ups and downs I've been through on this long road to creating success for my business and my family. I decided to write this book to share some of these exciting experiences, and to provide encouragement to those of you reading this, to encourage you on your own paths toward creativity and success in your chosen direction.

But back to Chapter 11, bankruptcy: it's not a pretty picture when you're suddenly confronted with a near-impossible business situation that threatens fifty-something years of your hard work. Although we had a thriving business, with close to *125* employees, through a series of mistakes, we found ourselves in financial difficulties. We had a cash flow problem, and we lost the support of our bank. In short, we made a lot of mistakes, which I'm going to tell you about in this book so that perhaps you can learn from the things we did wrong, as well as from the things we did right. What happened was that we didn't stay focused on what we did really well. Instead, we branched out, we got all these new ideas and tried to do them all at once because we knew there was a need for them. We grew too fast, which is probably the biggest mistake people make in any business. In addition to our successful products, we've had a few that laid an egg. And we've had a lot of things out on the market way too early. There's a thing called *timing* that is so important in our industry, or in any industry, and you've got to learn timing if you really want to make it.

When I've finally realized that we were over-extended and had to declare bankruptcy, nobody out there knew about it. People in our industry knew we were having trouble, but not the consumer, because we were still on television, we were still publishing our monthly magazine without interruption, and still shipping orders to our customers. But when you enter into bankruptcy, you find yourself facing lawyers, lawyers, and more lawyers, and judges, and court orders, and nervous creditors, not to mention hostile takeover attempts from other companies.

But quite often when things happen that you might think of as bad, they're not really bad: they're another opportunity, a chance for you to learn another lesson. Boy, I've had a lot of lessons! And a lot of fun learning them!

More than that: every major problem in my business, or in my life, for that matter, has led me to something good, in one way or another. And I'm sure that if you look back on your own life's many interesting twists and turns, I'll bet you'll see that the same holds true for you...

Tiffany asked me one day why I decided to write this book. There were three reasons, the first of which is that I'm sorry now I never really took the time to find out my parents' and grandparents' life-stories, and so I wanted to record my own story for my grandchildren, should they be interested some day in the future.

The second reason I decided to write this book was that for several years now I've had many people writing me letters, asking how I got started with Aleene's Tacky Glue. While they might know me from television, or from my many presentations around the country on behalf of the crafts industry, it seems that a lot of people have responded with interest about my manufacturing tacky glue more than anything else. For some reason, they love that tacky glue!

And the third reason I wrote this book is that I hope to inspire women, (and men!), so that they know they have the power to follow their own dreams. And make them reality...!

--Aleene

Aleene

Great Grandpa Evans & Family Group Photo.

Aleene with Papa Jackson, Grandma Nettie & Great Grandma Rebecca Evans. Rebecca was in her nineties at the time of this photo. My regrets that I didn't ask her about her life while she was still alive.

CHAPTER ONE

My Early Days

I think I'm the only person I've ever met who was born in Hollywood, California. My father, Frank Murrin Jackson, came from Calamity Gulch, South Dakota, and my mother, Vera Sophia Offerman Jackson, from Milwaukee. My great-grandfather on my father's side, Robert H. Evans, helped settle the town of Spearfish, South Dakota. It doesn't seem possible, but my great grandma met my great grandfather when her wagon train party was attacked by Indians. I have a copy of the newspaper at the time of his death, telling how he and a group rescued the party. They met and were married in Spear Fish. My great grandmother died when I was 15 years old. I had the opportunity to ask her about the Indian attack and her life, but at age 15, I wasn't interested. How I wish now I had been. My mother and father later met and got married in Great Falls, Montana, and soon after came to California to settle down. I was born in Hollywood, on January 20, 1924, on the cusp between Capricorn and Aquarius, just as the country was heading into what became the Great Depression of the 1930's.

At one-and-a-half years old I knew I was different. I always had a goal in mind, something that I was going to do. I guess I believed early on that goals are very, very important. Even if the goal sounds very pie-in-the-sky, I'm always willing to try something. Because when you try, something is bound to happen. It may not turn out as you had planned or hoped, but I believe in the old saying that if you don't try something, then you know nothing at all is going to happen. If you try, then at least you've increased your odds that something will be a success.

I was originally named Vera Aleene, but since my

mother used Vera, I always went by Aleene. I didn't like the name Vera and have never used it. Although my dad called me AL-leene, I have always called myself uh-lean, and I'm fussy about that. I try to correct people when they call me things like ALE-leene, or Arlene, or even Eileen -- I always say, "it's Aleene, like gasoline," which is the only way they get it right. It's a funny thing about names, because I've always believed that everyone should be free to choose their own name really. My daughter Tiffany, for example, was named Michelle, which became Shelley. But when she was 9 years old, she decided

Aleene about 3 yrs. old.

that Tiffany was the name for her, and it's been Tiffany ever since. My son who was named Frederick, became Rick for a time, then Von, then chose Fred. But names are such a personal thing, aren't they? We should all be free to chose the name that suits us!

One of my first goals, and one that got me my first spanking, was going across the street and down the corner to a little friend's house. I was not quite two years old and already I was very independent. In those days times were hard and it was common for large families to live together under the same roof. We lived with my grandparents and my aunt Lois, who was about ten years older than me. If anybody had a problem, you helped each other out, whether it was about jobs or paying bills. In fact, since my parents were

Aleene & Mom
About 1-1/2 yrs., the age I started to show independence by visiting a
friend down the street. This was my first spanking that I can remember.

away working, I was raised more by my grandfather, Frank Riggs Jackson, than by anyone else.

When I was about three years old, times were particularly hard. We all moved out to San Gabriel, about an hour east of Los Angeles, which in those days was fairly rural. An older gentleman, Timothy Drislane, had been looking for a family to help take care of him and his large house on an acre of land. My parents and I shared a bedroom, my grandparents and aunt Lois shared a second, and Mr. Drislane lived in a third. Occasionally relatives visited, so sometimes there were three or four families living under the same roof. In those days, all living together was totally normal. We had chickens and other animals, and everyone helped out. Another lesson I learned in those early years came when I was in charge of feeding and watering the chickens, and one time I forgot the water and some of them died. I've never forgotten to feed my animals or water my garden since that day. It was a big family scene during holidays when more relatives would come. And Thanksgiving, Christmas, Easter and July 4th, were always special. We didn't have much money, but we had a roof over our heads and food to eat and family.

Everyone was always doing something back then; fixing things, building things, sewing and making clothes, or taking care of animals and plants. My grandfather and father both, insisted on my joining in on anything they were building even though I was a girl, which was very unusual at that time. No one treated me like a girl except for my mother, who from the time I was one year old, out working and playing hard with my grandfather, insisted on changing my clothes every time I came in dirty, which was usually four or five times a day. In a way I was too much for her, and it was as if she and I both knew it from the beginning. Other than that, I was raised by the men.

I had no brothers or sisters, but my aunt, Lois, ten years older than I, was like an older sister. Lois recalled that I was sort of an ornery child, and often the only way she could get me to quiet down was to put me in the buggy and bump the buggy up against the side of the house. When I was a baby I didn't sleep too well, so my father would take me for a ride in the car, around the block once or twice, and that always worked. To this day if I'm in a car for a long trip I drop off to sleep instantly.

My grandpa was always building things. He built sandboxes, teeter-totters and lawn swings as a business. My grandmother was a seamstress who worked at home, but I guess at the time I was more interested in what the men were working on than in her work. I remember that my grandfather's death, when I was about nine years old, struck me particularly hard since we'd spent so much time together. I think I went into a kind of shock over it, but I didn't show them that it had affected me as much as it did. And then later, throughout my life, I developed a

Though I was an only child, my aunt Lois was like a sister to me.

similar kind of reaction - I always seem to appear as if nothing affects me. If it does, it's really deep down inside of me, and it doesn't show.

There was a family, the Bells, who lived down the street from us. We became and stayed friends all through the years since then. They had five children, and I loved going over to their house, especially on Friday nights, when dinner consisted of popcorn and milk, served like cereal. Then they would have hot buttered popcorn for dessert! To me, this was something special. I loved it, and still love popcorn to this day as a result. One night at their house I fell on a rusty nail, which made a huge gash on my leg. I remember that they poured some alcohol on it which stung like mad, but I wasn't about to leave and go home because it was "popcorn night!" In that day and age you didn't go to hospitals or doctors to get something sewn up, they did it right there at home. I still have a scar from it, but I sure remember that popcorn! I recall that Mr. Bell, the president of an electric company and a member of the prestigious Jonathan Club in downtown Los Angeles, was like a king in his home. And since he liked me, the kids were always happy when I came over because their dad wasn't as strict with them when I was visiting.

It was during this period that my grandmother became a psychic. Someone had given her a Ouija board, and she discovered that when blindfolded, she could point to letters spelling out messages guided from the other side. In so doing, she discovered a talent which a few years later she turned into a business in Los Angeles doing automatic writing for people.

My father was the patriarch of our family. I was the only one who would stand up to him and get away with it. He wasn't ornery or anything, he just knew how he wanted things to go, and did everything to make it happen as he thought it should. When my mother took ill, about ten years before she died, there was a time when she was down to eighty` pounds or so, looking like she could go any minute. But my father told her not to, so she didn't. He just said, "Don't die," and so she didn't. She hung on for another ten years.

As the "disciplinarian," my father would say to me, "Well, here's what I think about such-and-such a matter, but you can do anything you want. If it doesn't work out, you're responsible, I'm not going to help you." I liked that approach, it made me feel more mature at a younger age, knowing that I was responsible. And it always made me think twice about some of the stuff I was thinking about doing, because I knew he wouldn't help me if I did something outrageous and got into trouble.

Everybody talks about parents today as being a problem, or the cause of your problems, but I've never really understood that because I thought my parents were perfect for me. My mother didn't bother me, since she was very quiet. My father was a good example for me, since he would say, "Aleene, do what you want, but you're going to have to take the consequences," which, of course made me stop and think before I acted. I never knew that we didn't have money, but I always knew that if I wanted it, I had to make

Lois' wedding album. That's my father and mother on the left.
I'm the flower girl on the left.

it, because they didn't have it to give. But they gave me everything else that I wanted and were very supportive in other kinds of ways.

It's funny, but looking back on it now I realize I was sort of a "latchkey kid," but I didn't think anything about it. I came home from school and my parents weren't there, they were out working. I had some little chores to do, like cleaning the house, some gardening, and my homework, and I was happy to do them. I didn't give it two thoughts, because in that day and age, you just weren't naughty; it would never have occurred to me, because you were certain to get a spanking if you were!

We took a beautiful trip to Montana when I was about seven. It was in 1933, and large numbers of people were out of work all over this country. We had no money, but my father succeeded in earning money by painting cartops in a number of towns along the way. That was when cars had tops that were cloth or canvas, and they needed painting or re-sealing every few years. I remember that my father was usually working two or three jobs at once, everything from waxing dance floors to selling oranges and eggs, to working in restaurants, then managing and eventually owning a few. But in my childhood, things were very difficult for us, financially speaking.

In my early years, my parents weren't too religious. I think they attended a couple of different churches out in San Gabriel. My mother, who'd lost her mother when she was about seven, was raised in a Catholic convent. I don't really know what my father was, since he didn't ever seem too interested in religion. I can remember dressing up and going with them to a Christian Science Church a couple of times, and then to Unity Church. But a few years later, in around 1931 or '32, when I was about seven or eight and we were living in Los Angeles, we went to hear Dr. Ernest Holmes, founder of the Science of Mind Church. At that time it was called the Institute of Religious Science, and he had an office near Westlake Park, above Martini's Grille.

Dr. Holmes didn't teach about "God," but about "spirit," and I think it helped me develop a very positive approach to things. We used to go every Sunday, as did thousands of others, to lectures he gave at the Wiltern Theater in downtown Los Angeles. Dr. Holmes taught that everything was love. He talked about how life was tremendously abundant, and that when one door closed, another one opened. And that everything happens for a reason, that everything's a step in the right direction, even if it seems to you that it's not.

Later, when I was married and my children were small, we started going to the Church of Religious Science. We went to Church every week. Two of the children even went to Church School. I began Bible studies at a church in Alhambra, but I had a terrible time with it. I just kept saying, "why should I believe this?" And nobody could give me an answer. Finally the minister said, "I don't think you belong here," and I agreed with her. I've been against organized religion all my life, although I'm a great believer in Spirit.

You can be a very spiritual person, in my book, and not be religious. I have come to believe that everything is available from the Universal Mind. It's like electricity-- we didn't discover electricity, it existed and was operating before we humans discovered it and how to make use of it.

The same with the Universal Mind, it's always there, waiting for us to tap into it. The talks Dr. Holmes gave all those years ago were very inspirational to me. They inspired me at an early age to believe that you can do anything you put your mind to. And if this or that fails, it's a lesson leading you to something better. This has happened to me all my life. Everything I did just led me to something better, something a little bit higher. It's interesting to me that a lot of what Dr. Holmes was saying back then has become popular now. I guess good ideas get rediscovered and recycled with each new generation.

When I was eight we moved into Los Angeles. My grandmother had moved back there first, from San Gabriel, and we lived with her off and on for several years, between Westlake Park, now called McArthur Park, and Lafayette Park. I remember that I was always organizing the other kids who lived around the apartment into projects, like selling lemonade or other things. I was a natural salesperson even at age eight, and I think I was around nine or ten when I made my first little corsages to sell. I got some pansies from our apartment landscaping and wrapped them with tin foil from discarded cigarette packs. Then I went out on Wilshire Boulevard in Los Angeles, trying to sell them to people on their way to dinner or the theatre. I remember that I was so persistent at nine years old that many people started to worry that it might appear they'd kidnapped me, so they'd finally give in and buy my corsages!

At the time, I went to Hoover Street School, and they put me into an "Opportunity A" Class, which meant that they thought you were real smart. They called it an accelerated class, but it really wasn't. You were taught a lot of things, but not the basics, like math, for instance. I remember that I spent a whole year doing a report on Alaskan bison.

We didn't learn anything in those classes and I got bored easily in my early school years. The boredom continued on into junior and senior high. I later realized that it was an era when education was changing, though maybe floundering would be a better word, and I think I paid a price for it. And on top of that, I skipped 6th grade and went right into Virgil Junior High. Unfortunately, the year I skipped was the year they taught fractions, and without that, I could never get on with math.

My first learning to ride English Saddle with "Chico."
This started my love affair with horses.

This picture of me and "Billy" was taken during the time that I worked at the Griffith Park Riding Academy.

During junior high, when other girls were discovering boys, I discovered horses. We were living in an apartment house in Los Angeles, and one of the tenants had a relative, a girl from the Philippines, who came to visit once a year. She took a group of us kids out to Griffith Park to go horseback riding. She rode English-style, and I was so taken by it, that I tried to find out everything about it that I could.

I started going on the bus, two buses and a streetcar, actually, every Saturday morning, to go to horseback riding classes at Griffith Park Riding Academy. I loved it there, and soon I started going on Sundays too, when I could, arriving on the earliest bus and leaving on the last. In short order, I was living at the stable. When other girls, my friends, were developing crushes on boys and going to parties where they played spin the bottle, all I could think about was horses. Having no money, I was happy to work there, cleaning the stables, working in the office, anything to be able to ride with the other kids who went there and who were all very wealthy. It's a funny thing, but I've never had a sense of smell, and very little sense of taste. Evidently, when I was about four years old, I'd had my adenoids taken out, and that was what must have done it. I could be in the stables, working around manure, and never smell it. Many years later I saw a doctor who was checking my nose and throat, and he asked me about my adenoids. When I told him I'd had them taken out as a little kid he said, "you had a butcher, and that's why you can't smell or taste anything." Even though I love flowers and gardening, I've never really been able to smell the flowers. But if you've never had something, I guess you don't really know what you're missing.

By now I had graduated junior high, the shortest girl in my graduating class, and was trying to make my way through high school. I certainly wasn't what you would call a good student, getting some B's and mainly C's, because I was bored and just didn't like school. Nothing really challenged me. I could study, I could memorize, take tests and all that, but it just wasn't where I wanted to be.

And I was rebellious at what you'd call "an early age." I'd fibbed a little bit to get into Los Angeles High, telling the school that I lived at my aunt's address because I didn't like the school, for my area, Belmont High, which was in downtown L.A. I'm not proud of it, but I ditched school a lot. I just couldn't stay away from those horses and that stable. Lucky for me, the man in charge of the school's attendance office knew where I was off to, and he let me slide more times than not.

This was a picture of me in the Los Angeles High School era.

I did have a science teacher that I really liked who put a lot of focus on horticulture. I really loved that. I've always loved gardening, and even today, it's one of the main things I like to do.

My father was in the restaurant business from the time I was in junior high school. He managed the Tam O'Shanter Inn, a popular restaurant in Glendale at that time, and later he owned a few, like the restaurant at the William Penn Hotel in Los Angeles, and one at the Lido Hotel in Hollywood. I put in my share of hours, hosting and running the cash register, and I saved every nickel for the stables. I remember that my parents even gave me a quarter for lunch each day, and that I passed on lunch, adding the quarter to my horseback riding fund. And I didn't stop there. We had a switchboard on the main floor of our apartment building, and I volunteered to relieve the operator during dinner time. I was a quick learner, and still am, and I watched the operator for about ten minutes and quickly got it. In a short time, I became quite good at it.

Then, while in high school, I formed the Equine Club, for kids interested in horses. The actor, Victor Maclaglen, a movie star of the forties and fifties, was a member at the stables and he sponsored our club.

At that time, you weren't allowed to have a club that wasn't under school auspices, and the principal and I got into a real battle over that one. I felt that since it was sponsored by someone at the stables, it didn't have anything to do with school. The principal felt otherwise. He demanded that I make our club one of the official school groups, but I refused. He threatened me with expulsion, and said he would send me to a Catholic girls' school. I certainly didn't want that, but I held my ground. There wasn't much he could do about it, but things had gotten so bad between me and the principal that I ended up dropping out of Los Angeles High and spending the last half of the year at John Marshall High School, which is where I finally did get my diploma.

I was always organizing, whether it was clubs, or just people to do things. I remember I organized a dance for our Equine Club. I hired the orchestra, got the Riverside Drive Breakfast Club for the location, and got two or three hun-

I attended Los Angeles High School until I was kicked out.
Graduated from Marshall High School, 1942.

dred people to come. I probably got along better with adults than with kids my age. I felt I had more in common with adults: I loved to work and still do. If I'm going on vacation I want to go and see something, not go sit on a beach. I'm not that kind of person, I guess.

I was always questioning authority from an early age, even though I was really a quiet girl and didn't participate in many school functions. I didn't join the debate club or any of the other after-school activities that most of my friends did, and I almost never raised my hand to answer the teacher's questions.

When it came to public speaking, believe it or not, I was in the shy category. I remember that back then, as a schoolgirl thinking about her future, I dreamed of going into ranching, or some horse-related enterprise. Later, there was a time when I worked helping my grandmother as a receptionist. As people sat waiting for the psychic readings with grandma, I would write little poems and sell them to the customers. But I never felt that I was a writer. I even failed one class in English literature and had to repeat it.

My future husband Woody charms the girls! I'm second from
top right. This was used in the publicity poster for the Equine Club
Hawaiian Dance.

But what happened? My life turned out to involve
teaching classes, writing books and instructions, appearing
on television, lecturing, and public speaking to larger and
larger groups in the crafts world. Strange how things turn
out, isn't it? I'm recounting this to you because I want you
to know that in spite of the fact that I had very little educa-

Vic, my first real love because of our mutual love of horses.

tion, and that I did nothing through my school years that would have led me to this career, I was able to develop skills on my own, able to develop self-esteem and self-assurance, and to go on and create a large and respected enterprise. You too can develop the strength and confidence to follow your own dreams It's never too late.

One of the good things that did happen when I was in high school was meeting "Woody" Frederick Elwood Hershman, who became my first husband and the father of my five wonderful children. My girlfriend Denise Ware, we called her Donnie, was going out with Woody, and the three of us spent time together. She'd met him at his church, and when they started going together, she introduced him to me.

At the time, I was going out with a fellow at the stables named Vic, a multimillionaire's son. Donnie thought he was cute and he was going to inherit all that money some day. Vic loved horseback riding as much as I did, so we had a kind of romance going. But Donnie came up with a deal where we traded, though of course the boys never knew about it. She wanted the millionaire's son and I liked Woody.

After a couple of weeks Donnie changed her mind, but it was too late, since Woody and I were now dating.

Woody was two years older than I, and by the time we were going steady, he was at USC, and I was in my last year of high school. Woody's father was a respected doctor, the old-fashioned family doctor of years ago, very nice, but he had little to do with his kids because he was so busy. His mother was what we used to call "stuck-up," sort of haughty about her position in life. They lived in a beautiful, three-story colonial style house in Los Angeles, filled with expensive antiques. I wasn't exactly the "chosen one" for her son. For one thing, Woody was in college, and I had no intention of going. And I think his mother looked down on my hard-working parents. When Woody and I first were dating, I knew he wasn't that interested in horses, but he came along to be with me. He was a very quiet fellow, very artistic with loads of talent. But his mother was very domineering in his youth, and she did everything she could to control him, and to break us up.

At first, we used to walk home together from school, which was about five miles because I didn't live in the district. We would stop in at my dad's restaurant at the William Penn Hotel and get a chocolate malt or a soda. I remember he told me that when he was working afternoons at Ralph's Market during junior high, his mother always took his money away from him. His family was very well to-do, but it was just part of her trying to keep control of his life and his activities.

When all the other kids were getting bikes for Christmas, he wasn't. When his friends were getting cars, Woody got a bike. He always had a lot of beautiful clothes, but, obviously as I look back on it now, he never had the family closeness he wanted. Maybe that's why he became so reclusive, almost hermit-like. Later on, when we were married and in our own home, he could be sitting next to a telephone, and if it rang, he wouldn't pick it up. I'd have to come rushing in from outside to answer it.

I don't know; maybe it's true that opposites attract. There was always a big family scene going on at my house. My grandmother was one of eleven children, and all the uncles and aunts kept in touch, visiting from time to time, so there was always a lot of people around, and a lot of family warmth. But I'd have to push him, or Woody wouldn't have visited his family for Christmas, he was that disinterested in people.

Don't get me wrong. He was a wonderful person, but very private, very much to himself. He liked to read all the time, the kind of guy who could answer any of the questions on the TV shows, like "20 Questions" or "The Price Is Right." Woody was also the most honest person I've ever met. He didn't put on any airs, and he just was who he was. People who got to know him really liked him, but he was hard to get to know because he was so private--but super-smart.

Woody's family was determined that he become a doctor, but I knew for a fact that he couldn't stand the sight of blood. Once, we were at a rodeo and somebody's horse reared. The rider fell, and was cut and bleeding. Woody turned white and passed out. It was my father who finally persuaded Woody to let go of the idea of medical school (it probably didn't take that much persuasion), and get into something that he might enjoy doing. Dad knew that Woody was good with his hands and very creative. He suggested that my soon-to-be-husband go to flight instrument training school at Curtiss-Wright Technical School, a facility which wasn't too far from where we lived. My dad knew that Woody wasn't the type to go fight hand-to-hand, so he recommended the Air Force, which he eventually joined. After we were married, Woody became very close to my folks, and they loved him.

I remember that Woody was a fairly good dancer, although he didn't like to dance as much as I did. At one point, years later, when our company was growing, we started a dance group, made up of ourselves and our employees, and some of the vendors who'd become our friends. We held classes, everything from tango to cha-cha-cha, which gave me a great background in dancing. But boy, do I need practice now!

I remember that there were dances every Friday and Saturday night back when we were at Los Angeles High, and Woody and I went to as many as we could. I also got into Country Western, though at that time it was just called

We attended school dances most every Friday and Saturday night.
Pictured: B.J. Hines, me, Donnie Ware, best friends.

Western. We used to go to the Riverside Drive Breakfast
Club, or The Hitching Post in the San Fernando Valley. I still
enjoy Country Western dancing.

I remember the afternoon World War II started.
Woody and I were out at the stable, sitting in his car, listening to music, Glenn Miller or Tommy Dorsey. Then came the
news report on the car radio: the Japanese had bombed Pearl
Harbor. We both said, "My God, what's this going to mean
to young people, to people our age?"

I lived with my folks when I got out of high school
in 1942, and I'd found a job as a switchboard operator with
a company called Almquist Brothers and Viets, who were
jobbers in the field of industrial tools. Since the war effort

My first ride from Los Angeles to Santa Barbara with the Fiesta Riders.

was on full blast, the phones rang off the hook from morning 'til night. Every time the phone rang I had to say, "Almquist Brothers and Viets," a mouthful. But I was good at the switchboard, most likely from my volunteer experience at our apartment house in Los Angeles, and I also discovered I was faster at most tasks than other people. I worked there for about eight or nine months, but it got so busy that I couldn't take time off when I wanted to.

One day, I had the chance to go on a horseback ride from Los Angeles to Santa Barbara, a gorgeous five-day ride. It was with a group of horse people that every year rode from L.A. to the Santa Barbara Fiesta, then had the horses trucked back. I had the offer of a job taking care of the children in the group, and I jumped at the chance, saying good-bye to Almquist Brothers and Viets. The ride to Santa Barbara was well worth it. There were 200-300 people involved, and lots of children. We left on a Sunday, and reached Montecito, Santa Barbara's wealthy suburb, by Wednesday afternoon. We were hot and tired and dirty from three days' riding, but when we got to Montecito, we were joined by movie stars and other celebrities on horseback, "fresh as daisies," who led our parade into town.

When I got back I quickly found another job with an oil well equipment manufacturer, Kobe Inc., starting as a switchboard operator. The company made bomb-sights. One day the president of the company needed some help and asked if anyone would volunteer to stay late and do some letters for him. I was the only one whose hand went up. I wasn't a secretary then, but I did type well, and I was able to help him out in a pinch. As a result, he moved me from

"Trigger" was given to me by Ellis, a cowboy friend. "Trig" was a
champion quarter horse used for roping cattle.

switchboard into his office and gave me more secretarial
type tasks.

About a year later our family moved to Burbank,
and I got a job working for Lockheed, at Plant No. 2, down
at 7th and Santa Fe in Los Angeles. The war industry was
now working over-time, and I got a job on the graveyard
shift. I was the paymaster and timekeeper. Again, I did the
job three or four times faster than anyone else. The people at
the plant couldn't believe it. I started taking over for people
in other departments who were sick, or out for other reasons. I just buckled down and produced.

Another early job I had was at a restaurant called El
Rancho, which was near the Horse Bridge in Burbank.
People from all over rode horseback across the bridge over
the Los Angeles River to the trails. The El Rancho was interesting because it was a black-market type of place. When
you couldn't get butter or steaks, or even leather, because of
the war shortages, the people running the El Rancho
brought them up over the border from Mexico and sold
them at the restaurant. Bob Wills and his Texas Playboys

played there every Friday night, and that's where I caught the bug for western music.

Up until then, I'd been an Artie Shaw swing band type, but I definitely went "country." In fact, it was because of El Rancho that I ended up owning my first horse. One of my girlfriends had two horses, and she would come over to El Rancho with the extra one so I could go riding with her up in the hills. One day, a man came riding by, stopped to talk to us, and told us he was going to be having an operation and had to get rid of his horse. Would I take it? Would I! The horse was a champion, Trigger by name, and I kept him in the stable which was behind my parents' house in Burbank. Trigger was a quarter horse from the King Ranch in Texas, and was used for roping.

By now, Woody had found work with a company called Cal-Aero, a flight training center in Chino, California, for pilots who were getting ready to go off to action. All told, we'd broken up three or four times in the four years since we'd been going together, but for some reason, we decided to get married. Woody's family never fully accepted me though, and while they came to the wedding, none of his sisters even wanted to be bridesmaids.

Woody and I tied the knot at the Wee Kirk O' the Heather, on January 22, 1944, in a beautiful chapel filled with flowers and plants at Forest Lawn Cemetery, which has eight beautiful chapels. We didn't have a honeymoon, and for our wedding dinner, he and I went out to Bob's Big Boy restaurant; just the two of us, for my favorite, spaghetti and chili.

I was very taken with the bridal flowers, and then and there I decided I was going to be a florist, or at the very least, work with flowers in some creative way.

In a sense, the wedding was sort of anticlimactic. Only a year earlier, we'd broken up, mainly at his mother's instigation. She said she'd buy him a motorscooter if he would break up with me, and darn if he didn't take her up on the offer!

The night we broke up, I called Woody's best friend, Jimmy Stevens, who was also a good friend of mine. He came over and sat with me most of the night, helping me get through the breakup. Jimmy later died during the war when his airplane crashed in Texas. I remember that one night I heard a voice in my bedroom, a voice calling "Brat," which was Jimmy's pet nickname for me. He was the only one who ever called me that. The next day we heard that he had been killed in the plane crash. I've experienced it a lot since then, hearing voices, but that was the first time it happened to me that I can remember.

As far as Woody was concerned, I was so mad about his breaking up with me as a result of his mother's manipulation, that later, when we got back together and eventually married, it stayed with me, nagging me somewhere in the back of my mind. It was as if deep down inside I could never fully trust him. And for a long time I lived with that uncertainty, wondering off and on if he was the right person for me. I loved him, but I was never certain about him.

Aleene & Woody's Wedding.
From left to right, my mother-in-law Grace Hershman, myself, Woody, and my mother Vera Jackson.

Aleene & Woody, married January 22, 1944.

CHAPTER TWO

My First Businesses

It was because of the fabulous floral arrangement at our wedding at Forest Lawn that I went there to apply for a job. I was told that there were no positions open, but my request to visit the back room of the shop showed Murphy, the head florist at Forest Lawn, that I was interested. When I hung around all day to just watch how they did it, something impressed him and Murphy said he would make a position for me. My job, was cleaning thorns from roses and placing them in water.

I always remember that event when people tell me how hard it is to get jobs. From my experience over the years, it seems to me that if you show genuine interest, and if you're motivated and can convey that, you'll get hired. I know the job market appears difficult today in many parts of the country, but from my perspective as a business owner, I think it's difficult to find people who are qualified or really willing to work hard.

It just seems to me that if you study the company before you go to apply, so that you're aware of what they do, maybe know a little bit about their history and their products and, you'd be a lot more prepared when you go to apply for a job. Also, take a moment to stop and think about what you could do for them to increase their business, or to help them. Too many people looking for jobs these days want to know things like, "What kind of vacations do you offer?" or "How much does the job pay?" or "What kinds of benefits do you have?" Most people wouldn't have said those things in my day. I wasn't necessarily taught that, I just knew it instinctively. I just knew that if you wanted a job someplace, you prepared yourself before going in there and talking about it. Also, in those days, I would often tell an employer that I'd work for free for a week, just to show that I could do it. Of course, with labor laws nowadays, I don't think you could do that even if you and the employer agreed, which I think is really dumb! There are situations where there won't be a specific opening, but because you show a definite interest, you might well open a door to a job.

For three months I just watched and de-thorned. When I realized that I needed more hands-on experience, I went and applied at the Ambassador Hotel Florist Shop and was hired. Again, I was cleaning flowers and placing them in water. During this period I heard about a florist class being taught by Mr. Verne Jackson, no relation, in downtown L.A., and so I joined the six-week program. This, of course, made me fully qualified to open a florist shop. Or so I

Woody and I open floral shop, 1944.
Woody left for active duty so I managed the shop by myself.

thought.

My folks had moved out to the San Gabriel Valley, and on one of my visits to them, I stopped in at a florist shop in the town of Arcadia. It was a one-person operation, run by an older woman who told me she was planning to sell her store. The price she was asking was much too much, but it gave me the idea to start my own shop. On another visit I discovered that the army had just closed Santa Anita racetrack as an internment camp. A store became available and just like that, I took it. My father found an old florist's icebox, its owner having just converted from ice to refrigeration, and bought it for next to nothing. He hauled it home for me, and suddenly I had a real florist shop.

On Day One of "Aleene's of Arcadia Florist Shop," a man came in to purchase a casketpiece for a service the following morning. "No problem," I told him. Now, remember that I hadn't ever made a casketpiece, but I had watched. I got up early, I believe it was 4 a.m., to get the piece done for

The ice box, discovered by my dad, renovated and used in my florist shop.

a 10 a.m. service. Around 9 a.m. the panic hit. Putting together a large floral casketpiece by yourself was a little different than doing it with five or six helpers, pre-wiring the stems, tying the bows, etcetera. But I made it.

This was my first visit to a mortuary, and not my last. I never did like that part of the job. On that first visit the mortician told me to pin the corsage on the body in the casket. "Don't worry, you can stick the pin right into her," the mortician said, "she won't feel it." I guess because I looked so much younger than my age, with my bobby-sox and all, they felt they could tease me. But right then and there, I began to feel like I had chosen the wrong profession.

Things started to brighten up when a man came in for a table centerpiece for the 50th wedding anniversary he and his wife were going to celebrate. Again, no problem. I ordered yellow roses and prepared a lovely, long centerpiece for a table for twelve at the Sportsman Lodge. But I'd spoken too soon; two problems this time. On the day of the event, the yellow roses still hadn't opened enough to give color, and I had to make dozens of yellow bows to fill in.

Woody leaves for active duty, and says goodbye at Los Angeles Union Station.

And, when I delivered my beautiful masterpiece, much to my dismay, my creation covered most of the table and hung over all the plates! I had only minutes to rearrange the bouquet. I had no complaints, but I'm not too sure that gentleman ever returned to my shop. You see, I was either just plain stupid, or I had so much nerve (sometimes I'm not sure which) that I just went ahead and did things. And I learned by my mistakes.

It was around this time that Woody was called into active duty with the Army Air Corps, and sent to Amarillo, Texas. I remember taking him down to Los Angeles Union Station, where he was to take the train to Texas. Since he was going to be gone for a while, I moved into the little room behind my florist shop. There was a hot-plate and sort of a kitchen, and I had an old couch which I slept on. So I moved right in. I had wonderful experiences at Aleene's of Arcadia, operating the store by myself, making deliveries before opening, then at lunch time, and again after closing. My folks began helping out too, with my dad doing some of the deliveries in between his own jobs. I had to be at the flower market by 6 a.m. three days a week to buy the flowers, then get back to the shop to get things ready for the day.

When I opened my shop in 1945, flowers were very, very scarce. The Japanese growers had been interned at the start of the war, and their gardens were shut down. You would almost kill for flowers like white orchids for weddings. I had a friend at the flower market whom I'd call in advance, and he would see to it that I had most of the flowers I needed.

But getting the flowers wasn't the only problem. Since flowers were scarce, you could take a bundle of them to the car, lock your car, and when you were getting another load, the first would disappear. Taking my dog, Teddy, with me worked wonders. And Teddy, who was with us for twenty years before he passed on, became a fixture in my store. Everyone knew Teddy, especially the iceman.

One day, the ice man dropped a 25 lb. cake of ice

Teddy, my constant companion
for 20 years.

about two inches from Teddy's nose, and from that day until the day I bought a real refrigerator, Teddy and the iceman had a problem. Teddy was very protective, and I never worried about being alone at the shop. One step toward me would bring out a growl from Teddy, and even though he was just a big Teddy Bear, no one wanted to test him. One time, however, Teddy was in the back room where I lived, laying on my cot, with his face resting on my purse. There were a lot of cus-

After one year I remodeled the Florist Shop with permission from the owners of the store.

tomers in and out that day, and later in the afternoon when I went back to my room, my purse was gone. Someone had evidently sweet-talked Teddy into letting him or her take it. So much for my watchdog.

So many wonderful things happened at that shop. As I began to learn about my customers, I found that many of them grew beautiful flowers, using them in their homes, and making corsages and centerpieces themselves. So I, as the budding entrepreneur and young businesswoman, began to sell them professional florist wire, florist tape, florist-type water-resistant ribbons that they couldn't find anywhere else. I made a good markup on the materials and was soon doing a very good business in these items that no one else was selling. In fact, I had people from all over California coming to me for florist supplies. Eastern Star ladies came wanting to make their own installation pieces, and many other talented women who wanted to create their own centerpieces and corsages. I didn't know there was an unwritten law that you didn't sell floral supplies, but I soon heard about it. The California Floral Association tried to discredit me as a member. They got so mad at me, they tried to kick

The ARCADIA FLORIST is pleased to inform you that we have changed our firm name to

Aleene of Arcadia

that we have enlarged and remodeled our Arcadia store; that the quality of our flowers is now better than ever and that our service is especially planned to please you.

To best express your perfect taste—your thoughtfulness —may we suggest flowers by

Aleene

of Arcadia

Phone ATwater 7-1000   26 E. Huntington Drive
Arcadia, California
We telegraph flowers anywhere in the United States and Canada.

This postcard was sent out when I remodeled the store.

me out. I got an attorney and I won. At this time I modern-
ized the store front.

Another great thing that happened while I was running the florist shop was my discovery of Styrofoam®,
which the Dow Chemical company had just introduced, and
which they were showing to the wholesale flower market. At
that time, Styrofoam® was just a flotation material. It had
never been used like you see it today. I just felt that there was
something exciting about it, but nobody else did. I went and
bought everything the salesman had for my florist shop. The
next day, my dad cut it into shapes for me. I believe he was
the first person who ever cut Styrofoam® into shapes in this
country, and later on, he developed machines for cutting
Styrofoam® into cones, balls and egg-shapes, which would
become so popular in our industry. At first, I made
Christmas centerpieces with it, and they went over big. Then
I cut a stork out of Styrofoam® for a baby shower, and the
people just loved it. So we started talking with Dow
Chemical about what we could do with their product. Later

My remodeled store. Note new florist refrigerator. Now Teddy no
longer needed to threaten the ice man.

on, my father developed machines to do the cutting and to fabricate Styrofoam®, and out of that we started a division of our company called SnowFoam. Ultimately, I became a spokeswoman and consultant to Dow on that new product. I did a lot of television for them, and wrote the first two books on what to do with Styrofoam® for the crafts industry. So every little thing led to something else.

Although I had learned about being frugal from my family and about not wasting money all the time I was growing up during the Depression years, at the florist shop I really began to learn about budgeting. I don't remember ever being aware that there was a depression on when I was in my childhood. Then it was natural for people to save, to work hard and to budget, so I guess it was ingrained in me without my even being aware of it. I realized that to run my small florist shop I needed to have a certain amount of money in the account in reserve. Though I had to buy new flowers three times a week, I never knew what was going to come up, a funeral suddenly, a special birthday bouquet or other last minute things.

HOLLYWOOD — Do you know that bubbly white plastic stuff that decorations are made out of at Christmas time? Now, it seems that foamy stuff is used to keep homes warm in the winter and cool in the summer. Styrofoam, as it is called, is a polystyrene plastic that has been expanded 40 times. The result is a foam-like mass of millions of air tight non-connecting cells . . . a near perfect insulating agent. It's being made in plank form and is one of the most practical and economical methods of insulating residential as well as commercial and industrial buildings.

But getting back to its decorative use, one girl who calls herself Aleene, has built an extensive and successful artificial floral and fibre business around the use of this material in do-it-yourself kits.

If you are interested in how Aleene makes her Christmas and floral decorations, you can see her on the Panorama Pacific television show on November 1, channel 2, 7 to 9 A.M.

I was the first to use Styrofoam® in the floral and craft business.

Money was tight. I ate beans for a year, and my folks

invited me over for dinner every now and again, just to be sure I was eating! But I started doing better and better, because I did a lot of extra little things that nobody had done before. When someone bought a box of flowers, I tied a corsage on top and didn't charge them for it, things like that. Another thing I did was to get artificial flowers and use them in my window displays. Nobody was doing that then, but a lot of people liked the idea and started copying it.

I was still running the shop when Woody came back from the service. But not for long, as I got pregnant with my first child, Candy, fairly soon. I had wanted children, and more than one, because I love children, and because I had been an only child and missed the closeness of brothers and sisters.

I put the florist shop up for sale and sold it to a gentleman I had met at the flower market. He came from a family that had specialized in growing roses, and was himself a very talented florist. But he didn't do very well because all my customers were used to me selling them floral supplies, and he wouldn't do it. Also, I'd built up a rapport with my customers. I've always liked people and gotten along well with people from every walk of life. I probably follow up with people more than the average person does, and I'm always surprised when people tell me they've lost touch with friends they had from years ago, because I sure try not to.

*

When Woody came home from the war and I had sold my shop, we bought my folks' place in Rosemead. The house was old, and when it rained the water came running down the driveway and right through it. Later my father and Woody built up the floor with some cement which kept the rainwater out. People nowadays would probably call it almost a slum. It was like a re-done chicken coop. Actually it was attached to the house in front, and had three very large rooms, probably 30' x 30', and we took one and

My "chicken house" home in Rosemead. I held my first floral classes
here. Note the tree roses down the driveway. I have featured tree roses in
every home that I have lived in.

turned it into a sort of family room. To add to it, we put in
a fireplace, making it really homey. We made the other two
rooms into apartments.

After they sold us the place, my folks bought a trailer and took my grandmother and my aunt on a six month
trip around the U.S. It was right after the war, and my dad
had a great big Buick 8 to haul the trailer. I have fond memories of that old Buick, since most of my girlfriends learned
to drive in it.

When my folks took off on their big trip, however,
they left me with about 5,000 chickens to take care of. That
would have been fine, but about a month after they left, the
chickens came down with chickenpox. At the time, my dad
had been selling them to Knott's Berry Farm, and since I had
no way to reach him by phone, I didn't know what I was
going to do about it. Finally the guy who was picking up the
chickens said to me "I can't sell these to Knott's Berry Farm,
but we can sell them to some other people." I said fine.

After our first daughter, Candy, was born in 1947, and I had sold my florist shop, I started teaching classes from my home. Women came from all over for classes in wedding arrangements, Christmas designs, funeral work, and a variety of other things related to decorating and flower arranging.

I started selling some of the florist supplies to them from home, since they still weren't available to retail customers in florist shops. Some of the adult education schools heard about my classes and asked me if I wanted to teach through them. Did I? You bet! As I've said, each thing seems to lead to the next thing, and with the classes, I was starting to reach more and more people wanting to learn about flowers and floral crafting. They immediately gave me an adult education teaching credential, and pretty soon they had me teaching all over the greater Los Angeles area, including places like Long Beach, El Monte, and all over.

Teaching those classes was good money in those days, and what's more, they allowed you to sell your products, which I did. My second child, Fred, was born in '48, so mom helped out with taking care of the two little kids while

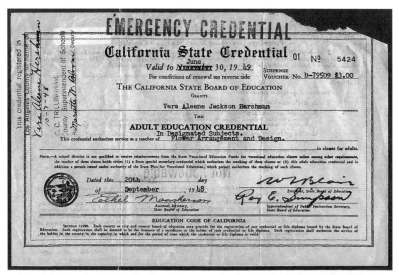

My Adult Education Credential to teach floral arranging and crafts in school.

I pursued my Adult Ed teaching career. I got around a lot with those classes, and more and more people became familiar with what I did. In addition, I was an "Avon Lady" selling products to friends and acquaintances.

Selling Avon was great because I could take little Candy with me in the car and then in a stroller as I went door to door. The thing I learned from selling Avon was that I was a really good salesperson. I didn't like selling door to door, mind you, but I was good at it. I remember that when I got my territory up, Avon promptly divided it in half, and brought on another girl. We've been doing that lately with my company, so I know how my people feel. But it's something that happens all the time in sales, so you get used to it.

From all the excitement about my selling florist supplies to my students, I got the idea to develop a "Make Your Own Corsage Kit." I felt that if people could buy a kit, with everything needed plus instructions (the flowers, of course, they would supply out of their own gardens), it would be a hit. Remember, I hadn't had a lot of English or writing classes when I was in high school, so when I wrote my first set of instructions, I kept them very simple. And I think that helped a lot.

Putting together the "Make Your Own Corsage" kit really gave us a hands-on education. We had to design the box, write and print the instructions, put the whole package together, and then go out and market it. Around this time, Woody and I bought a used mimeograph press, and he did some drawings for the "Make Your Own Corsage" booklet, the first of hundreds. Then, when the corsage kits were ready, I went out and marketed them to nurseries and department stores in Los Angeles; places like the May Company, the Broadway and Robinson's. As long as I personally demonstrated them, the corsage kits sold. But they never set the world on fire.

Business was picking up for me though, and pretty soon I had trucks pulling up to the back of the house with fairly sizable deliveries. As I recall, the neighbors started to

My first attempt in starting a business - Aleene's Make Your Own Corsage Kit.

My first attempt at advertising. Here's a Department Store ad. I also did in-store demonstrations.

complain about all the commercial activity, so I began to think about renting a place. We lived in what could have been considered a dumpy location, so I can't imagine that the neighbors were really bothered by it, but they were. Again, adversity led me to something better.

Around this time, I got the idea to go on television with my "Make Your Own Corsage" kits and some other things I had been using in my classes. Don't ask what inspired me. At that time television was just in its infancy, and there were only 300 or so TV sets in all of Los Angeles! I didn't have a television set and neither did any of my friends, but that didn't stop me.

I knew about TV because about six or seven years earlier, probably in 1942, I had seen it being previewed at the old Ambassador Hotel on Wilshire Boulevard. During the Easter Parade in Los Angeles they'd set up a television camera and monitor and were showing people what television could do in the very near future. It was amazing to see. We take it for granted today, but for us back then it was like going to the moon would be for a later generation.

Somehow, in 1951, I got hold of the people at KTLA, which I believe was L.A.'s first station, and talked my way onto a show called "Handy Hints," run by a gal named Dorothy Gardener. She liked what I was demonstrating and invited me to appear once a week.

Each week I would show something else

My first TV appearance, with Dorothy Gardener on KTLA. At the start, the audience consisted of only 300 TV sets.

about working with fresh flowers or I would plug my corsage kits and the stores or nurseries where you could go and buy one. When I'd been on the show for a couple of months, there was a company selling TV sets at the television studio, and I bought one. We were suddenly the hit of the neighborhood. Ten or twelve people would come over in the evening and we would all sit together and watch TV on a 7" set. That's right, I said a 7" set! But it was thrilling nonetheless. During the time I was on KTLA, people like Gorgeous George, Spade Cooley, and Stan Freeburg had shows. No one probably remembers these shows today. It was so long ago I have trouble remembering myself. But I know that I enjoyed those shows, and that it was the start of my appearances throughout the years on TV shows, that helped to sell my products and give me recognition.

Because of my early appearances on the "Handy Hints" show, I decided to buy time on another station, KFI, another early Los Angeles television station, and start my own show, "Fun With Flowers," It ran for about thirteen weeks. Through that show, I met Gordon Baker Lloyd, a gardener who also had his own show on KFI.

Gordon suggested that our talents could merge together well. He would teach the viewers how to grow flowers, and I could show what to do with them once they

This show on KFI was the first show I produced and starred in.

were grown. I joined forces with Gordon and he taught me about public relations. He was having all kinds of special classes and getting lots of publicity for himself, and he taught me some of the finer points of how to do the same. And because of him, I developed my own special knack for getting publicity for my products and classes.

Gordon taught me how to talk to people, how to reach them, and how to get publicity for your project, product or organization. One of the main things I learned, which I'm passing on to you readers is don't pay for advertising when you can get free publicity. People don't read the ads, but they do read the stories. So try to get your free publicity by writing publicity "releases," little stories which you submit to the editors. Of course, what I was doing at the time was new and different, and there were lots of stories to write about. But I believe you can publicize anything for free, if you go about it the right way. Think about what is unique about your project and write something short about that. Look for the angle, as they call it, where you can attract a reader and an editor's attention. Also, since local cable TV has to originate some programming, if you have any talent (make that "nerve"), why not contact them to do whatever you do well? Whatever you are enthusiastic about, whatever you would like to teach or share, take a chance, take the

A very important group. From left to right: "Hilda" who introduced me to Formosan Wood Fibre, my mom, Gordon Baker Lloyd who gave me TV and PR experience, myself, Gordon's daughter and a student.

risk, and above all, be yourself!

*

We rented an old winery building on Valley
Boulevard in the town of Rosemead. We had a little retail
shop at this location, selling florist materials, ribbon, wire,
tape, and Styrofoam®. To increase sales and people's awareness of what I was doing, we started having "open houses,"
which at the time was rather new to people.

One winter I had a class on making corsages, and
there weren't many flowers to arrange or to do anything else
with. One of my students, a woman named Hilda, brought
in something called Formosan Wood Fibre. She had had it
stored away for a number of years, and since we were using
fresh leaves, candy, anything we could think of in lieu of
flowers, she wanted to share this wood fibre with the rest of
the class. I saw right away that this material was something
special. It came from a plant called *aralia papyrifera* which
grew on the island of Formosa, and it looked very, very natural when glycerin was added to it. Adding dyes, you could
make flowers with it, flowers whose petals were so soft they
seemed like the real thing.

That night after class, I showed the fibre to my dad.
By coincidence, he had sold some machinery to the man who
was processing the Formosan Wood Fibre up in Yucaipa,
California. The next day, Dad went and bought $15.00
worth from the man and brought it back to me. I started
showing it in my different classes and everyone got really
interested. And so, little by little, I bought more and started
selling it, both in my Adult Ed classes and to people who
were coming to the winery building to buy florist supplies.

Soon thereafter, I got the exclusive distribution rights
to Formosan Wood Fibre for the twelve western states. The
packages at that time retailed for a quarter, but little by little they went up in price and peaked at $3.95 a package. A
lot of the older people in the crafts world will remember me

Hilda and mother waiting on customers.

for the Formosan Wood Fibre, as much as for anything I did later on in the industry.

It was around this time that one of my contacts told me about a man in New York City, Bob Valliere, who sold all the things I needed for artificial flowers, and so I began a correspondence with him, to find out his prices, what he had, etc.

In order to make Formosan Wood Fibre flowers we needed other supplies as well as the fiber; things like the stamens, the center of the flowers, and Bob's company, Signagio & Co., in New York, had them. Signagio & Co. also sold me the little pips and all those little things that you find in artificial flowers, such as flower centers, stem tubing, and things like that. I came out with instruction sheets on how to make a hundred different kinds of flowers; not just roses, but carnations and magnolias, and just about every flower imaginable.

After we'd been doing business for a time, I flew to

Aleene and Gordon Baker Lloyd promoting fresh and
artificial flower arranging. Featuring: Aleene's Formosan
Wood Fibre.

New York with my dad, to meet Bob. He was working out
of a great big loft making artificial flowers for hats and
clothing. He had beautiful, great big roses for the hats. He
was importing from Germany and Poland, and he had materials which I hadn't seen before.

His aunt, Miss Signagio, had been in the millinery
business making flowers for years. I spent a lot of time talking with Bob, and learning as much as I could about how to
make this into a successful business. He also made the silk,
satin and velvet petals that I was to buy for my customers.
In a way, this was the start of my really being in the wholesale business. Remember, I'd been just a retail store. But little by little, through word of mouth, people found out that I
had more than just wood fiber, and I started having store
owners come to me. Suddenly, we became a wholesaler.

I was now selling a lot of the Formosan Wood Fibre,
and more and more people were getting interested in it.
Everyone in the family was working at other jobs, but they

pitched in to help with the baby-sitting, or with different things. My mother would take care of the shop when I had to go off to the Adult Ed classes, and I remember that we were so friendly with most of our customers that we often just let them ring up purchases on the cash register themselves! Later on, some of my better customers came to work for me when our business expanded.

One of the fun things about the early days of this business was that people were so excited about it that they just kind of volunteered. For a long time, as I recall, we didn't have to pay people. They would just stay and do anything they could to help out, enjoying themselves the whole time they were "working."

I think the main thing I did that put me squarely on the road to success was to be able to see the right things to publicize. And remember, since I didn't know that I couldn't do something, I always tried. And I was always highly active in whatever I was into.

Mother and I traded off babysitting and working in the store.

The first show I promoted was the Floratrade Show at the Biltmore Hotel in Los Angeles. My dad gave me a budget to work on. The show featured Wood Fibre, flower making materials and designs. And our many vendors participated with us. It was a very successful show.

At the Los Angeles County Fair I displayed our products for about three or four years. I belonged to the Southern California Hobby Industry Association, and became active with them, working my way up to vice-president. I did a mountain of publicity work for the Hobby Industry Association; things like getting them on television at KTTV for two years on a show called "Hobby Corner."

On the show, I did fifteen minutes of crafts, and fifteen minutes of model airplanes and railroad-type items. Then I arranged free space at the Tabery Hobby Show for hobby and model and craft products. I was always promoting the Association and the industry as a whole. Later, with my friend and fellow pioneer, Hazel Pearson, we arranged for the Los Angeles County Fair to construct a "hobby building," as a permanent site. I directed the project for three years during the month the fair was open. The Association at that time was made up mainly of presidents of major toy and model companies, such as Mattel and Revell, and they had never had a woman as president of their organization. Well, you know me, or you should by now, and I screamed about it, until finally they caved in and accepted me as their new president. And this was long before

This shows a small portion of the Floratrade Show, held at the Biltmore Hotel in Los Angeles. Because of TV, thousands attended this first show.

The Petal Pusher

Vol.5 No. 6   June, 1956

Your Floral Design Newsletter

Aleene's Floratrade Show

August 24th, 25th, 26th
BILTMORE HOTEL
Los Angeles, California

Aleene Dealer's are co-sponsoring the "Floratrade" Show to be held on August 25th and 25th.

While this is primarily a dealer trade show, it will be open to the public on Friday and Saturday, August 24th & 25th from 1 p.m. to 10 p.m.

Plan your vacation in Los Angeles at this time and see Aleene Dealer "Prize Winning" Displays, Manufacturer's Display of new products and new uses for old products, continuous teaching and demonstrations on the latest floral techniques.

Tanner Bus Tours to the Aleene's Temple City headquarters. Ask your dealer for further information.

Bottle Arrangements

When arranging in small-necked containers, arrange the flowers and foliage in your hand before placing into vase or bottle. It is much easier than placing individual flowers into neck of bottle.

Use dried materials and weeds for height. Picture shows treated Wheat, with dried Dock (weed) and dried Watsonia leaves. Add a few flowers (5) for focal point. Baby zinnias of No. 532 fibre pasted to No. 508 fibre were used in the arrangement.

The "Petal Pusher" was a monthly newsletter of the Aleene's Fibre and Floral Supply Company. the Petal Pusher offers design ideas and special events.

there was anything called women's lib!

Another thing I learned in my early days in business was not to spend money when you don't have it. This may sound simplistic, but I think that most people fail because they save up a lot of money and then sink it all into something, and it just doesn't come out the way they thought it would. What we did was to start small and just grow slowly, seeing how the new product went, increasing it as needed, but not spending where we didn't have to. And don't forget, we all worked jobs on the side for money to live on while we were building up our business.

We very quickly outgrew the winery and bought a building in Temple City, California, on East Las Tunas Drive. This was to be the home of Aleene's Fibre & Floral Supply Co. for almost twenty years. The company was officially incorporated in 1948, but the crafts industry didn't really even exist yet. It was around this time that my father and my husband both quit their jobs to come work with me.

Aleene receiving a plaque from the
Hobby Association of Southern California.

Shown, a small segment of the hobby craft building that I was responsible for at the Los Angeles County Fair.

After that, one uncle left his job at a car dealership to come and work as our bookkeeper, while another uncle joined us to take charge of the wholesale side of our growing business. My mother came in to handle the mail order sales, and, before too long, the whole family was employed in the business which I had launched from the family room of our rebuilt chicken coop in Rosemead.

My own kids started out in business running the cash register when they were four or five years old. They worked after school and during the summers. It's been a family business ever since, going on fifty years as I write this, with four of my five children actively involved in running it.

People say working with your family members is very difficult. But you know what? It's no more difficult than working with other people. At least your family has a real interest in it. You argue. Sure, my son Tony and I argue. He's the one I finally put in charge of the business. He's the youngest, but he's the most like me. He's more business-minded than the others. The others are more artistic, and he's more business. My daughter Tiffany has developed her business side producing and hosting our television show. But my kids were on television in their early days, running the cash register when they were so small they had to stand on a box to operate it, so they've grown up with this business.

The new building we got was an old furniture factory, so it had lots of space to develop the different aspects of Aleene's Floral and Fiber Supply Co. The building had an upstairs, where we had the offices, and the retail sales were down in front. The wholesale department took up about two-thirds of the back area of the building. We had already started importing all kinds of gadgety-type things from other

Moved to a new building in Temple City, California. Note each one in our family had a matching stationwagon.

countries, that could be used for Christmas corsages, tree-trimming, and gift package decor. Dealers began coming to us and wanting us to sell supplies to them, and so I started giving them classes on Sundays on how to use the materials.

Grandma Jackson, "Gee-gee," teaches a class.

It grew and grew. I also did a lot of garden shows, like the one at the Los Angeles County Fair. I brought artificial flower materials and displays and things like that. I wasn't sure of the reception I'd get there among the people selling real flowers and flower arrangements, but I went anyway and was elated when people came crowding around my tables at the fair.

By this time, I'd had my third child, Heidi, born in 1949, and our business was starting to take off. In addition to the classes and the products, we had developed a whole division of Alcene's fabricating Styrofoam®, a Dow Chemical product, which we called Snow Foam. I was always looking for new products to add to our existing lines, especially when I realized that sales of Formosan Wood Fibre were starting to level off. I developed as many different kinds of flower materials as I could, and we got very heavily into the Styrofoam®-type products, including party materials and lots of kids' crafts made from the white stuff which was becoming so well-known. I started kids' craft classes on

Saturday mornings and they became quite popular.

As our business increased, we added new products and printed new materials to go with them. We sold our original mimeograph machine and bought a multi-lith offset press. I wrote instruction sheets on basic flower making with Formosan Wood Fibre, giving detailed instructions for such beauties as Wild Primrose, Apple Blossom, Violet, Carnation, Delphinium and Camellia. Woody did beautiful drawings for these instruction books, and he developed pho-

This was the first fresh flower show that I attended featuring artificial flowers. We were surprised at the wonderful reception. The Wood Fibre looked so real.

tographic skills as well. He also took in outside printing jobs for a while, but we had more and more printing for ourselves, patterns, idea sheets, catalogs, things like that. And after a few years, we went from the multi-lith press to a big Harris press to handle all the work. In short order, our publishing department took off all on its own.

Writing this book has reminded me that one of the best suggestions I can give you is to consider writing about your own experiences, or writing "how to" do whatever it is that you do best, or whatever it is that you are passionate about. Remember that I had never written much in school, was a very poor student in English, didn't like literature, and yet one of the most profitable and successful things that I have done throughout my life has involved writing. I started with that "Make Your Own Corsage" booklet. Not having a large vocabulary was a plus for me, as I kept the instructions simple. When I look back on those early books we did, as compared to the books we have been working on lately, I still see very informative work which gave the instructions clearly, allowing anyone to follow them and to succeed.

Submitting articles to your local newspapers or magazines can be a rewarding experience for you, whether they get published or not. Keep trying! Don't feel that you have to be a professional writer with college degrees, just simply write about something you know, something that has happened to you or something you wish to share with others. I can't emphasize this enough-- have confidence, have faith in what you're doing, in your vision, and then act upon it. Go forward, one way or another. As long as you're pursuing your goal, you can't be doing wrong. And even if you go down a dead-end, turn around, re-evaluate, and then go on some more. Believe in yourselves-- and others will too!

Here is a sample of our first instruction sheets that we printed. Please note in the center, our first printed booklet.

As we grew, we progressed first to, single-color 8 page books, and then to a 1 color cover, 8 page books.

A FAMILY AFFAIR.

From left to right standing: Uncle Claude Epp, book keeper, Cousin Richard Epp, Dad, general manager of Aleene's Fibre and Floral Supply Co., Woody, Cousin Bill Jackson, wholesale manager. Seated: Myself, Mamma Jackson, Gee-gee, Cousin Bea Jackson, Aunt Ann Ingalls, Cousin Lois Epp. This was a Family Company Christmas Card.

CHAPTER THREE

The '50s, the Family, Television and Me

I don't want to keep repeating myself, but it has been true for me that one thing just seems to lead to another. I guess I'm saying this because it helps if you keep your eyes open to see just what it is that you're doing now, and what it may be leading you to in the future.

The sales of Formosan Wood Fibre brought me to silk petals from the New York company. The silk petals caused me to look for a special glue that wouldn't soak through the silk. Originally, we used a gum arabic to put the pieces of wood fibre together. But to work with silk, you need a glue, that won't soak through or all you'd have left would be a little wad of glue in your hand. We tried different glues, including one called Wilhold, and then Elmer's, but none of them worked right. So I went to the chemist at the company that was supplying me glue at the time, it was called Arabol, and I said to him, "Can't you make me a better glue? One that won't soak through every time?"

A couple of weeks later he got back to me and said, "I've got something, why don't you try it and see if you like it." I did, and it turned out to be the forerunner of Aleene's Tacky Glue, which has been and continues to be our best selling product. In the beginning, I called it Glue D'Aleene, and marketed it that way. But we had about twelve designers working for us then, and I'd hear them say, "Pass down the tacky glue," or "That glue's sure tacky." And so, little by little, I changed the name to Aleene's Tacky Glue, and it stuck-- no pun intended.

What was more amazing was that the man who had

Joe Magdaleno was my first salesman for the Arabol Company, and
has been with me for 30+ years
since the start of Tacky Glue.

created it, gave me the exclusive rights to the formula. At first it was a verbal agreement, but when he sold his company to Borden, he gave me the rights in writing. And it's true what they say, always get it in writing! Later on, I had to fight Borden Chemical Co., because they kept trying to copy our glue using that formula. They brought it out once under the Elmer's name, and my attorney contacted them about it. He told them that if they wanted to come out with a glue like ours, fine, just pay Aleene's the royalties for the product. It seemed for a while there that we fought this battle every two years or so. Borden's kept changing managers in that particular department, and the new ones would see how popular my glue was, and wanted to come out with a similar product, or at least one that worked as well on silks and satins.

I don't remember how it came to me, but I decided I wanted a gold bottle for Aleene's Tacky Glue; something that would make it stand out from other glue products. It cost us more to produce the gold bottles, but it was worth it because it gave my product a special look. In fact, if anybody copied me with a gold bottle, we were able to stop them legally as the law reads that another company can't mislead the consumer into thinking they're buying the original. Although many have tried. At one point, someone came out with something called Sticky Glue, instead of Tacky Glue. It wasn't the word "Sticky" that bothered me, it was that they'd come out with a gold bottle. All I had to do was find three people to say they were confused by the product, and we would have a legal leg to stand on. Needless to say, we won the case. It's been over thirty years since we introduced Aleene's Tacky Glue, and today it has more than 90% name recognition over all other brands in the field. At present, we've got three companies formulating it for us. And if someone tried to copy it today, it wouldn't make too much difference because we've got a name for ourselves that everyone knows from many years in the business. None of our competitors have come out with anything like it; it's that unique.

*

I don't know whether or not I was born a marketing person, or if I acquired the know-how, but I do know that it can be learned by watching, listening, and asking the right questions. If you have an idea, a potential product or service, think it through carefully, and write down some notes for yourself about it. Specifically, write down why you would buy that product. Ask your friends about it, would they buy it? For how much? And for what reasons? Packaging the product is, of course, very important for sales. Look at other products on the market, products designed by very talented, highly-paid people, and incorporate their ideas into your packaging if they are appropriate. Be certain that you protect yourself by checking with a copyright or patent attorney when you're ready to go to market with your product. This is one of the necessary costs. When I had very little money and couldn't afford a patent attorney, I used to send an idea to someone or some company by registered, certified mail. At the same time, I'd send the same letter to myself, also registered and certified. I would keep it un-opened, so that in case at some time in the future I had to prove that I had submitted that idea to the person or company, I'd have a U.S. Post Office official record of the mailing.

When you have an idea that you think is good, research it to find out what company could use your idea along with their other products. They're always looking for something to add to their line. Having an allied product allows the salespeople for the company to sell it at the same time as they're presenting other products to a customer. And write to trade organizations for information on the type of product you are proposing. Try to find out what is happening in that particular industry or service sector. This will help you in selecting someone or some company that might be interested in your idea. But don't forget that the best information you'll get will be "in the store." There you'll be able to see what your product or idea might be competing with. You'll also get a sense if there are any related products that might correspond to yours. Those would be the companies you'd do well to contact. Above all, try to do the best you can at every step of the way. I remember a story about Ben Hogan, the golfer, who was being interviewed by a journalist right around the time he was at the peak of his championship career. "Mr. Hogan," the young reporter asked, "has luck played a major part in your success?"

Hogan looked thoughtful for about a minute, then replied, "You know, son, it's the damnedest thing, but I find that the harder I work, the luckier I get."

I told you something about my start in television in the last chapter, but since it has played such an important role in my life, I want to tell you more about my experiences with TV. In 1951, when I started as a guest on that first show, Dorothy Gardiner's "Handy Hints," KTLA had only been on the air for about a year. Dorothy specialized in talking about home furnishings, linens, dishes, and things like that. She brought me on to talk about flowers and arrangements and how to make them. Since KTLA was a part of Paramount Studios, the station was located on Melrose Avenue in Los Angeles, just outside the Paramount lot. It was quite an experience for me from many standpoints. The lights

I guested with
Art Linkletter on CBS.

were really hot and the makeup was caked on. It had to be almost orange-colored to make you look normal. And it was live. If you made a mistake, you just covered up as best you could. Videotape didn't even exist at that time.

For almost a year, I was a regular guest on Dorothy Gardiner's show. Then I started a self-produced show on another new station, KFI, which was on Vermont Avenue in downtown L.A. Cadillac Co. owned KFI and they were quite happy with my first daytime show, "Fun With Flowers." On the third show, I remember, all of a sudden I lost my train of thought and I froze, like a deer in the headlights, with nothing to say for about five or six seconds, though it seemed like hours to me. I've never forgotten it, but I also never let it happen again.

From there, I went on with Gordon Baker Lloyd, developing my television presentation skills and learning about public relations. At the same time, our business was expanding, I had three very young children, and so all in all I was quite a busy lady. I stayed on with Gordon Baker Lloyd, learning things about the television business which itself was only just beginning. Then I moved over to KECA, which is now KABC, and I bought the time to air my show, "Fun With Flowers." We weren't yet taking orders from television viewers as we would later do, so I merely showed them how to use our products, and mentioned which stores were carrying them. I was now on all by myself, which was a lot different than guest-appearing on other people's shows.

I also did guest spots on other shows, like the AM Show, Red Rowe, Regis Philbin, Betty White, and Art Linkletter. Later, after getting my feet wet with my own show, I had enough gumption to approach Tennessee Ernie Ford, who at that time had probably one of the most popular shows on national TV. As I've said earlier, a lot of times I just did something because I didn't know that I couldn't do it. I approached Tennessee Ernie's company with the idea of showing them something you could create with egg cartons, and they accepted me for the one show. At the time, I was heavily into promoting what we then called "junk crafts," using available materials like egg cartons and such. But remember, there was no crafts industry in the early '50s. What there was were individuals throughout the country

I guested for a short time on the Al Jarvis Show
featuring the now popular Betty White.

who practiced crafts, some of them making and selling products and supplies, but there was virtually no "industry" to
speak of. After that one appearance on Tennessee Ernie
Ford's program, the show received over 100,000 letters from
people who'd enjoyed it and who'd tried what I had shown
them. So they asked me back, and again there was a flood of
mail after my appearance. Shortly thereafter, I was invited to
become a regular on the Tennessee Ernie Ford Show. Since it
was taped in San Francisco, I would fly up once a week from
Los Angeles and stay overnight in a hotel. Then I would
spend the whole next day in the studio because Tennessee
Ernie would tape five half-hour shows in one day. He had
wonderful guests on his shows, as any of you who are over
forty will recall. Jack Jones was introduced to audiences that
year on Tennessee Ernie's show, and a whole lot of other per-
formers who went on to become quite famous because of
TV. Those were an exciting two years for me, flying to San
Francisco and back every week. But I loved traveling, and a
good thing, too, because as our business progressed, I began
to travel quite a bit. And Tennessee Ernie Ford was a really

I was a paid regular weekly guest on the Tennesee Ernie Ford Show for two years. Two of my best years on television as Ernie was the nicest celebrity I had ever met. And the other guests on the show were really interesting too!

good person, one of the first of a series of what we used to call "show people" I met and worked with.

Next came the Gypsy Rose Lee Show. When Tennessee Ernie Ford went off the air, his producer moved over to Gypsy Rose Lee's, and got me onto her show. She was living in Beverly Hills at the time and on quite a few occasions I would go over to her great, big house. It was messy, with clothes all over the place. She loved crafts and sewing. I guess she sewed her own costumes. It's funny, she wasn't terribly attractive in the conventional sense, but she had a wonderful personality, and she certainly appreciated the work I was doing. I think I was on about a year when Gypsy died, and the show along with her.

Then came Tom Frandsen, on NBC, who insisted I be a regular guest on his popular program. In fact, it was Tom and his show, two years later, that helped make our first Crafts Caravan in Pasadena a great success. Because of the publicity through his show, our first Pasadena event drew more than 20,000 people! When our Crafts Caravan-- more about this later-- started out on the six month trek around

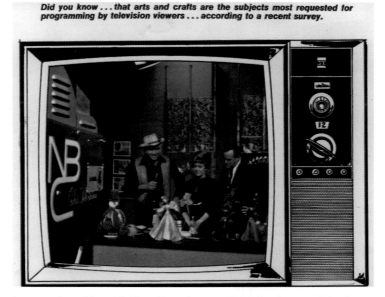

Appeared weekly with Tom Frandsen on NBC for 2 years. Met interesting guests such as Lorne Green, star of "Bonanza."

EXCITING TELEVISION SERIES

video taped in beautiful color

19 five minute, educational, entertaining "how to"

segments are available to insert

in your existing programs.

an ARTS and CRAFTS SERIES called

ARTIS, a designing woman

Each segment is filled with fun projects that the viewer can create, not only from craft materials but from "junk."

Tom and I created 19 five minute segments that were syndicated on 143 stations throughout the United States. Note: This was during my Aurora fiasco and I was going under the name Artis/Aleene since I couldn't use my name during this period of time.

the country, I would fly every week from wherever I was to Burbank Airport to make my appearance. Then I'd fly back to where the Caravan was and rejoin them. As I recall, we did two shows a week for six months. Plus one or two days per week I'd have to train the local associates who were helping us with the Caravan, then fly back to where Tom Frandsen was, and then fly back again to the Caravan. Whew! Just remembering it tires me out. And yet the Crafts

Caravan really primed the pump for the birth of the whole crafts industry.

As I traveled around the country promoting our Crafts Caravan and our company's products in general, I would call local stations before my trip and set up interviews with them in advance. Usually, newspapers and television or radio stations in those days had what they called the "Women's Section" editors, and they were more than happy to book me for their programs, or to do interviews for the newspapers. After a few years of my calling, they started calling me for guest appearances. In recent years, I've had shows on the Learning Channel, Lifetime Television, and currently, "Aleene's Creative Living with Crafts" is on The Nashville Network five mornings per week.

Speaking of media, one great boost to our efforts came in 1953 when *Life Magazine* did a spread on the family and Aleene's Fibre & Floral Supply Co. The article was on America's fastest growing companies, and we were recognized by them for helping to spur the growth of the

For many years I guested on morning shows, noon shows and women's shows in every major city in the United States.

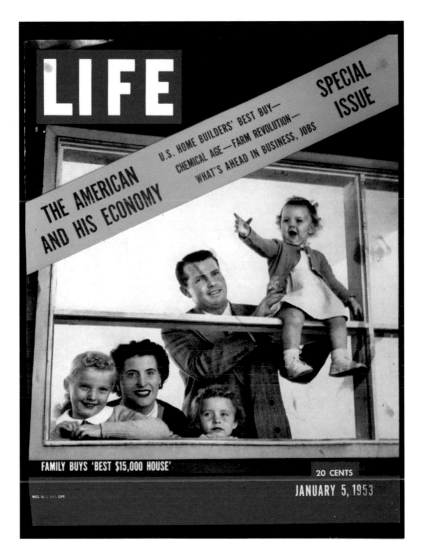

Aleene's was featured in Life Magazine, - January 5, 1953, as one of the fastest growing companies in the United States.

Year after year a growing number of Americans have traded off the almost universal daydream of striking it rich in a business of their own for the more immediate reality of job security and the luxury of letting someone else worry about meeting the payroll. Many are discouraged from stepping out on their own by high taxes which take so much out of profits that it becomes difficult to plow enough back into the business as capital for expansion. But bucking this trend, there is always a band of adventuresome folk who take the risks of self-employment for the potentially richer rewards it holds. Even with all the spirit they can muster, however, the going is rough. In 1951 three out of five of all U.S. businesses which failed were less than five years old.

Some who have lasted and become modern money-makers have, like the young engineers (right, top) and the ex-schoolteacher (right, below), capitalized on technology. Others, like those on pages 96 and 97, are quick to cash in on new merchandise and merchandising methods. Some, like 28-year-old Aleene Hershman (opposite page), pyramid hobbies into profits.

As a youngster in Los Angeles, Aleene used to slip out to florists' trash cans, pick up old posies and peddle corsages on Wilshire Boulevard. Four years ago Aleene lost $1,200 in a mail order business set up to sell corsage supplies, but a year later she came across some Formosan wood fiber, found it ideal for making artificial flowers and bought $12 worth. In 1952, selling the materials from which housewives and hobbyists can make artificial flowers, Aleene's Fiber and Floral Supply Co. grossed almost $1 million and took care of the employment problems of most of her family (below).

YOUNG ENGINEERS

Just a year out of engineering school, Wilbert Choy (right) and George Foster (center) decided in 19__ to produce for industry a laboratory measuring device using radioactive strontium-90. With Wilbert's brother Roy (left) they had only $600 of their own

In the feature article, "Money Makers of a New Era," *Life Magazine* wrote "Some, like 28 year old Aleene Hershman, pyramid hobbies into profits."

Life Magazine says "despite taxes, they take risks and profit from their own businesses."

Aleene's family poses for *Life Magazine*. Aleene, Woody,
Momma Jackson, Grandma Jackson, Papa Jackson, Aunt Lois
Epp, Uncle Claude Epp, Aunt Bea, Uncle Bill Jackson and
"Teddy".

American crafts industry. At the time, we were grossing over
a million dollars a year in sales, and this was something
unusual, for a company headed by a 29-year old woman.
There was a beautiful photograph of me with our realistic-
looking wood fibre roses, and one showing the whole family. Since *Life* was probably the most popular magazine at the
time, millions of people saw that article and I know a lot of
business came to us as a result.

Don't forget that at the time there still were no crafts
companies as we know them today. There was American
Handicrafts, a company specializing in leather and related-
products, and only a few mail order-type companies, but no
retail crafts stores to sell to. What did exist was the Hobby
Industry Association, focusing on model airplanes and
trains, but crafts as an industry was just barely being born. I
think that *Life Magazine* article sure helped some in the
birthing process. And today, crafts is a multi-billion dollar
industry in both this country and around the world.

Adversity. Everyone in business, and certainly in life

in general, faces adversity. I remember hearing a saying, something like "That which doesn't kill me only makes me stronger." And it has certainly been true in my case. As I write this, we've just successfully come out of a two-and-a-half year bankruptcy proceeding, a fascinating (and occasionally harrowing) story which I mentioned in the introduction and which I'll tell you about in a later chapter. It wasn't easy, and it wasn't pretty, but we pulled together and stuck it out, and now Artis/Aleene's Inc. is back on the road to increased profitability.

Things were moving along pretty good for us when fire struck on June 19, 1959, destroying one of our buildings on East Las Tunas Drive in Temple City. (See next page for picture.) Starting with a faulty electrical connection, the fire burned up about $100,000 worth of floral merchandise, and obliterated the wholesale and mail order departments. Our retail store was completely destroyed as well. It took about five or six hours for a team of about fifteen firefighters (we called them "firemen" in those days), plus a couple of big fire engines, to finally put out the blaze. Only the records of the business were saved. The fire was centered in the Wholesale Department and completely destroyed the ceiling and the roof of the building. Typewriters, heaters, desks and miscellaneous office equipment just melted from the extreme heat of that fire. But before the day was over, our family and friends had gathered to plan our survival. We organized our selves to operate from a new warehouse next door, which we'd just been getting ready to open. Everyone got busy contacting the insurance companies involved, the contractors to help rebuild, and the equipment companies to order new machinery to keep us going. At the time, we had a professional class made up of dealers who were coming to learn about using our products, and we just shifted it to my house and kept right on going. We quickly transformed our other warehouse into a classroom for the general public, and my office became the retail store. What had been the print shop offices became our Retail Shop for a while, until we could rebuild and start all over again. And that is exactly what we did.

It took a couple of years to get back on top, but we did it. At that time, in the late 50's to early 60's, we were sell-

Aleene's Burns!

Firemen don Oxygen masks to locate source of flames. Dense smoke hampered efforts along with high flamibility of materials.

...ding goes up in ...wasn't destroyed ...ruined by smoke or ...xtreme temperatures.

In the midst of debris plans were made for a new, beautiful Retail Store.

The fire centered in ... Wholesale Departm... destroying even the ... ing and roof of the b... ing. Typewriters, ... ers, desks and m... anous office eq... melted from extr...

...cup of fire finishes the job, and ...stairs offices. Only the records were ...noon of the day of the fire, plans were ...ontinue "business as usual" in the new ...se, next door. Contractors, insurance ...and equipment companies were busy pre- ...Aleene's for continuing business this ...r and for rebuilding and reopening in ...mber.

Classes were continued as usual. A professional class that was in session was transferred to Aleene's home. The Print Shop was transformed int... a temporary classroom for summ... Retail was re-established in the Pr... ing offices.

Faulty wiring causes major fire damage in one of our two buildings. Thanks to the help of our employees, friends, family, and suppliers we were up and shipping in a few days.

After the fire, we rebuilt the building. We lost the roof, all of the merchandise and the entire contents of the building.
Note: our new store front.

ing Styrofoam®, which was growing and becoming its own division called Snow Foam. My dad had been cutting Styrofoam® into a variety of shapes for a number of years, making designs with leaping reindeer, or storks for baby showers, that kind of thing, and he'd also invented machines to do the cutting. People would use the Styrofoam® for the character part of the arrangement, then put flowers at the base of it. We sold Styrofoam® of all different sizes, including one that was a three-foot long piece that looked

Though I started Aleene's, and brought my family to join me, Papa Jackson was president. My job was design and promotion.

like snow. It was about an inch thick, and my father had cut two reindeer and a sleigh out of it. We were also selling all of our flower-making materials, the silk and satin petals, and we were only first getting into glue which we were selling to individuals and some of the earliest crafts-related stores. At the time, it was still called Glue D'Aleene, but I had a feeling about it, an intuition that this glue could really become a popular product, since there was no other product precisely like it on the market. Formosan Wood Fibre sales had leveled off, and it seemed to me that people's interest in that product was waning. I was hot to develop new things, in particular, the glue. But then I came up with some unexpected opposition, my family.

As I mentioned, in addition to my father and my husband, there were uncles and aunts and other relatives by marriage who were intimately involved in the running of our business. My father and the rest of the family wanted me to go out and promote Formosan Wood Fibre, even as sales were starting to slide. The wood fibre came from the island

Which one has the "Tony"? Can you see which one is real and which one is made from Wood Fibre?

of Formosa, and was packaged by a company in Yucaipa, California. We represented that company, and were exclusive distributors for the product in eleven western states and Texas. It was cut in squares and packaged in sheets about an inch thick. When it first came from Formosa, it was white and very stiff and would crack easily. The company in Yucaipa, Raymont & Co., would mix it with a glycerin wash which would soften the wood fibre. Then they colored it. They would do things like two-tone it by coloring it, say, all yellow, then putting a clamp in the center where the yellow was. They would then put a red dye in the center, so you'd have a variegated color to it. Some of the colors were solid and some were splashed, which gave them the look of real flower petals. People would then buy the squares, take them home and cut them into the flower petals as they wished.

My family was sure that since it had been a good selling product in past years, additional publicity and promotion, would get sales back up again. I believed that we had to go into new products, that the wood fibre had had its day, and that it was time for us to move on. I guess in the back of my mind I couldn't stop thinking about that glue and its possibilities.

The family kept insisting on their point of view, saying "Aleene, you're such a good promoter, all you have to do is get out there and promote the wood fibre and sales will go back up again." Nothing I'd tell them would make them believe that it was going down in sales and wasn't going to come back up. We had a meeting, actually more than one, and it got argumentative and quite heated, as those kinds of things can get. After a few of those meetings, which I knew weren't going anywhere, I said to myself. "Well, I think I'm gonna have to get out of this, because I just don't see any future in it." I couldn't convince them that it was time to move on, and they couldn't convince me to go their way.

We decided to split up, the family and me. I had the fantasy of going to northern California and buying a small newspaper and running it. And I'd found one that interested me. But my dad came up with a solution, proposing that they would take Snow Foam, and I would keep Aleene's Fibre & Floral Supply Co. They were going to continue fabricating Styrofoam® products, while I would start again and rebuild Aleene's, this time with just Woody and myself. Talk about adversity! The splitting of the company meant that my personal income had been cut in half. I still owned about 45% of the other company, Snow Foam, but now I wasn't going to be drawing any salary from it. In breaking the company into two, they took with them about a third of my business, and almost 100% of my help. I stayed in the location we had rebuilt after the fire, while Snow Foam moved out to another building, and not long after that, to an even bigger location. My cousin had also joined them at that time, and he ended up running Snow Foam along with my dad.

Don't forget that my father had been doing most of the managing of our business, while I had been involved in writing books and instructions, doing design, television, promotion and marketing. So while dad knew the ins and outs of handling the reins of a growing company, I didn't. But I sure learned fast. It was a very rough time for me and for Woody, too. We'd had our fourth child, Tiffany, in 1955. So between starting over again with my business, and four little children, I had more than a full plate, as they say. One of my uncles had been the bookkeeper and another one managed the wholesale department of my business, so when they both left with the family to go run Snow Foam, I had a few additional "adversities" to contend with. All of a sudden these very important and time-consuming jobs, bookkeeping and wholesale distribution, were dropped in my lap. For a while there it was hectic, as the whole of Aleene's, Inc. consisted of Woody and me.

You might think that things were really strained between me and the rest of the family, but that wasn't the case. I've always believed in family and in the strength of the family unit, which I think has been one of the biggest things going for us on television today. People love the fact that our shows are a family affair. You have problems in families, that's only natural, but you work through them. My father continued to give me advice and general suggestions as I managed my own company without him. My uncle, the bookkeeper, helped me in deciding on a new bookkeeper, and after a couple of tries, we found one who stayed with me for twenty-five years. My other uncle, who'd run the wholesale department, had had a fellow who worked for him and that guy came to work with me, so that was a help. Conversely, they still called me in for consultation on things related to design and packaging and promotion of their Styrofoam® products.

But suddenly, I was shoved into handling the financial part of my business, which was something that I just hadn't done before. And when you take that much away from a going concern, like a third of the business, your finances go through a major change. All of a sudden I had to run the business on a strict budget. That was probably my first experience of the difficulties in getting a business back on its feet. It was necessary in order to do what I wanted to with the company. But I set my mind to it, and through hard work and grace, and Woody's continued support, I succeeded.

I think how a person reacts is the key to most things in life. Something comes along and it looks like it could or should hurt you-- like when my family, led by my father, who'd been my most trusted advisor and supporter, decided they wanted to go a different way from what I wanted. Another person might have caved in to the majority's ideas, or just folded her tent, in response to such personal opposition. But if you change your mind about what's happening, and don't allow yourself to see it as being hurt, then you can minimize the hurt. It may even help, as has so often been the case in my life. Of course it's hard-- whether it be a death, or the loss of a business or profession-- it's hard, but you can control the hurt. It's your mind, don't forget. So the faster you get over it, and take hold, and do something about it, that much sooner will you be on track again and on to the next event!

One of the things I'm trying to do with this book, and with future projects I have in mind, has to do with empowering women. I believe that most women like myself weren't brought up to be successful. Thankfully that has been changing in the last two or three decades. I know I'm probably a lousy wife, because I've always had a million things I wanted to accomplish, and staying home being a good wife and mother twenty-four hours a day wasn't really on my agenda. If you want to, and you like to stay home and mind the home fires, that's great and I applaud you! I think it would be lots of fun to raise a child and really enjoy that child, forgetting the dirty dishes, forgetting about the house, really having fun and discovering the world with that child. That to me would be great. But the mothers who stay home and hate it, don't ever get a chance to express themselves, and that, in my opinion, is terrible. No matter what you want to do, do it and do it well. I was lucky, because the way I worked enabled me to really enjoy my children when I came home. I really enjoyed taking the children on trips. I recall that we had some neighbors who couldn't stand their children. These neighbors would leave the kids and always take vacations by themselves. I always took the kids on our trips because I really was able to enjoy them that way.

Speaking of trips, of which we had quite a few, Woody was the kind of husband who left everything up to me, from the first idea of a trip, to the details, to finally the packing. He was so disinterested, that only after I'd planned everything and gotten every little detail together, maybe an hour or so before the trip, I'd ask him if he wanted to go-- and then he'd say, "Sure," and go with us.

I was lucky, too, in that I had the same housekeeper,

Woody and I bought an old airport bus and converted it into a 34 foot land cruiser that slept ten people. Since we had been working for Congressmen John Rousellot, we had been invited to visit Washington D.C. We planned for a one month trip. When we were driving through Oklahoma, the bus threw a rod, forcing us to continue our tour by Greyhound, train and airplane. We sent the bus back loaded on a truck. We traveled with sleeping bags as our luggage. You can imagine the surprise of our Congressmen John, when we arrived with sleeping bags. We enjoyed a wonderful stay with John and his wife Marilyn in Virginia. Having all the advantages of a congressmen, including parking our car in the red zone, and attending for "Congressmen only" special events.

The entire family loved our cabin at Lake Arrowhead. This was one of the few places I could really relax, feeding and taking care of my five children and their five friends that we had visiting us at the cabin.

Audrey Moore, a wonderful woman, for many, many years. I met Audrey when I sold some property to her, next door to mine. One day she came over to help me out with the kids and ended up staying for seventeen years. Audrey didn't have any children of her own, so I was very lucky in that regard. She became a second mother to my kids, and I know they've always felt close to her. But I don't think that it's necessarily luck, since I believe we attract what or whom we need at the time that we need them. She was great with the kids and enjoyed life with them. It added to her life and certainly added to mine. Audrey did a lot of things with them, making costumes, and generally encouraging their particular pursuits. I'm the one who kind of had to get after them, but they sure enjoyed her. The right thing or person always seems to turn up, if you let it.

Woody was really great when the kids were younger and he did a lot with them. Unlike a lot of couples, Woody and I never fought. We never even had a harsh word. He was good to me, and I was good to him. He let me lead the type of life I needed, and vice versa. I let him be what he was. And since we were starting to make a lot of money at that time, we bought everything he wanted, from a Porsche to boats up at Lake Arrowhead. My father had given us a house at the lake, and we loved to go up there with the kids for boating and fishing. But inside, I guess I was always wondering bout my marriage, wondering and feeling as if something were missing.

When you get married, I think you never really know whether or not you're choosing somebody for life. I know that I grew tremendously through the early years of our marriage, but in another way, I always felt that Woody was already formed, that he just was the way he was from the start. He should have gone to art school, he was that talented, but his father had wanted him to be a doctor, as I mentioned earlier in the book, and I think that colored how things went for him. As it was, we were growing in two different directions, and later when I fell in love with someone else and wanted a divorce, everyone who knew us was surprised.

Aleene and Ray Ramont. Ray did the final processing of the color, glycerine and final packaging. The wood fibre was cut and sized and shipped to the U.S. from the island of Formosa.

Hawaiian leis and other tropical designs were popular and made from Formosan Wood Fibre.

Merry Christmas

The Hershman Family
Woody, Aleene,
Candy, Ricky, Heidi, & Shelley
1959

Note: "Ricky" is now called Fred, "Shelley" is now known as Tiffany. I have always felt that kids should be able to choose their own names.

CHAPTER FOUR

One Door Closes, Another One Opens

Throughout the late '40s, when we were first promoting Formosan Wood Fibre and operating our retail business selling floral supplies, there weren't any retail crafts stores. They just didn't exist. What did exist were individual craftspeople, working from their homes. In Southern California, many people would start by taking classes, and they in turn would begin teaching in their circle of friends or family. My own family, of course, was instrumental in spreading both the word and the concept of home crafts, and even two of my cousins, after spending time with me and taking my classes in Temple City, went ahead and brought crafts up to the Northwest, opening "Pat & Bobbie's," a crafts teaching and product-distribution center in Seattle that has helped spread interest up there.

It was a very "grassroots" movement in those earliest days, with individuals making things for themselves, then a neighbor or someone at church would see it and ask to learn how to make it or how to do it. I remember one lady from San Jose who came all the way down to Temple City for our classes. Then she went home and started giving her own classes in her garage. She would order our products for herself and her students. And that's how it began to grow, with people passing it on to other people.

Some of those same people who'd started with crafts classes in their homes would decide to get into business themselves, opening a little shop in their town selling the crafts supplies they were getting from me. From there, throughout the mid-50s and into the 60s, the crafts industry

Hazel Pearson.
If I was the "Mother of crafts," Hazel was the "Grandmother of crafts."
This picture shows Hazel involved in copper tooling, taken at about the
time that I first met Hazel.

really began to develop. People, like my good friend and fellow pioneer Hazel Pearson Williams, offered classes and products throughout Southern California. Unfortunately, many of the individual creative crafters who started in their homes, said "great, we'll start a business with it," but they didn't really take into account all that goes into running a business. They didn't realize that the rent, the bookkeeping, and taking care of the store, tied you down, and often isn't any fun.

It's funny, but nowadays, the circle is turing, from craft chains and independent craft stores back to people working out of their homes. To begin with, so many of the chains have gotten into the field. Giant companies, like Woolworth's, Walmart, and chain stores such as Ben Franklin and Michael's, have forced a lot of small independents out of business. Ben Franklin stores, which used to be five and dimes, got hit by Walmart so hard that they've shifted more into crafts and party goods. But unless they were in a town that didn't have a Walmart or a Ben Franklin, the small crafts stores have been closing their doors in the face of corporate competition.

Speaking of Walmart's, which is now one of our biggest customers, I met Sam Walton a number of years ago, at a time when I wasn't selling to to his company. Only a couple of people in the crafts industry had been selling to him when I ran into one of his buyers, a fellow named Keith Haynes, whom I'd known from another business. Keith told Sam that I was the most knowledgeable person in the craft industry, and I heard back that Sam wanted to talk to me and see what I had to say. As a result, I flew back to Arkansas to meet with him. I'd been told that he was going to give me a half-hour, which itself was unusual, but I ended up talking to him for several hours. I was really intrigued by the man, and I got to where I knew him pretty well.

Before I met Sam Walton in person, I wasn't that interested in selling to him. Keith Haynes had been after me to get our products in their stores, but I really wasn't interested. I felt at the time that the big stores weren't necessarily good for the craft industry. But then, when I met Sam Walton and talked to him at length, I realized he was one of the greatest people I'd ever met in my life. We developed an acquaintanceship, you might say, and after that first meeting, I would go back every year to a show that he had. Sam would rent huge tents, and would bring in many of his associates from the crafts field. There's a great, big craft show down South called War Eagle, to which a million people come each year. At the same time as War Eagle, about 15 or 20 miles from that show, Sam would set up these tents and let his associates use them. Then, he would have a tent and have us in there doing demonstrations.

There were six or seven different companies represented when he first started doing these events. He would

From the Desk of Aleene

Since you are involved in the Craft Industry now, I thought you might be interested in attending this Craft Market show in Florida.

Perhaps you could schedule a visit in your Navajo, to your Florida Stores in conjunction with the show.

My husband and I would like to have you join us for breakfast, lunch or dinner. He too is an airplane aficionado. He is retired from our business, but owns the Maintainance facility at the Santa Ynez Valley Airport. He has built a Whitman Tailwind, is currently redoing a Taylor craft and is restoring a Convair World War II airplane.

Thank you,

Aleene

Thanks - Aleene - DEC 8 1985 Say I will

✻ **Artis Inc.** *Best wishes* *Sam Walton*

Mailing: Box 407, Solvang, California
93463 • (805) 688-7339

I felt privileged to have personally known Sam Walton.
Though extremely busy, his notes to me were always
hand written, not typed by a secretary.

have us for dinner and breakfast. And he always sat with me, because by then we sort of knew each other. Then he had me come back and talk. Fred and I visited his organization once in Little Rock, and Sam had the managers and assistant managers come in while I talked to different groups, so they could learn what I knew about the crafts industry.

Sam Walton was very down to earth. He was just a simple businessperson who lived in the same house he'd always lived in. He drove the same pickup truck he'd always driven. He didn't wear a suit. He wore jogging and tennis clothes, and was just plain friendly. He had a breakfast on Saturday mornings. Sometimes when I was there a day or two before, I would get up real early and he would be at the motel dining room. Everybody knew him. They'd just say hi, and talk about who won the ballgames and such. He had a very special quality that you don't see too often, a kind of humility and greatness both at the same time.

So now, as I write this in 1996, we're seeing a return to home crafting more than ever before. These are the people we call professional crafters, people who are teaching or making things in their homes to sell at art or craft shows. The chain stores aren't creative, but these professional crafters are. Unfortunately, we lost a lot of the creative people when the independent crafts stores shut down. So, the return to crafts as a business run from the home, is what is happening now, a full circle from the early days.

In our case, the sales and growth of Aleene's Fibre & Floral Supply Co. came about mainly because I would get out in front of people, doing shows like the ones we used to participate in, like the Hobby Show at the Shrine Auditorium in Los Angeles for the Southern California Hobby Industry Association, or the many country fairs and garden shows we did, as well as word of mouth, and of course, my television appearances. I think the biggest impact in getting the crafts movement off the ground was the Craftsmaker Caravans I organized in the late '60s, which I'll tell you more about in the next chapter.

In one sense, crafts and craftmaking are thousands of years old, dating back to the first caveman and cavewoman, I guess. Certainly crafts are as American as apple pie. When you think about the early days of this country and what the first pioneers had to go through. In recent American history, however, like in the 1920s and 30's, even into the early 40's, crafts were limited mainly to schools, recreation departments, and summer camps. Originally, "handicrafts" as it was called back then, were principally crocheting and stitchery for women and girls, taught from mother to daughter, and wood burning and carving for the men and boys. Before there was a crafts industry as we know it today, there was only the American Handicrafts company, specializing in leather and leather-working tools, or mail order companies that featured mostly stitchery kits, and that was about it.

Then, in the early years after World War II, the hobby-model industry started taking off with the popularity of plastic model airplanes and model railroad trains. And for a while, our efforts to spread the word of crafts fell under the wing of the "hobby" industry, especially since both Hazel Pearson Williams and I were very active members of the Southern California Hobby Industry Association. As I mentioned earlier, I'd worked my way up to vice-president of the SCHIA, though I had to fight like the dickens to get them to accept a woman president, me. But they finally did. The crafts field was a lot more than a hobby, and people soon came to realize that it was an industry unto itself.

If I was the "mother" of the crafts industry, my good friend Hazel Pearson Williams might be properly called the "grandmother" of the industry. Hazel, who was living and working in Temple City when we first got our location on East Las Tunas Drive, started out by teaching craft courses in local Southern California colleges, with a focus on copper tooling. She made simple patterns anyone could follow, and slowly but surely word of her work, and her products started to spread. Hazel, who as I write this, is now eighty-two, is a very friendly, out-going person, and we became close friends right away. After all, as two women pioneers in a field which was only just being born, we gave each other strength and support in more ways than one. She popularized something called "fried marbles." Marbles, probably the most popular children's game at the time, would crack when you fried them. And you could create things with them. I seem to recall that I was working with feathers and velour crepe paper around that time, and Hazel and I would get together and compare notes, so that we wouldn't both be selling the same thing against one another. A little later on, Hazel developed paints for her customers before I did, but hers were in jars. So I went ahead and created mine to be sold in spray cans.

But we worked together so much, especially later on with the nation-wide Craftmakers' Caravan, that people for a long time thought we were in business together. Hazel continued on, more as a distributor and a manufacturer of kits, while I became a manufacturer of products, such as glues and paints, as well as a distributor. I remember that I had her as a guest on several of my television shows. And we've remained close friends over the forty-some years that we've known each other.

In looking back on it now, I suppose I was the more aggressive of the two. I always argued with people and tried to push for things, while Hazel was happy just to go along. Hazel went on to the board of directors of the national Hobby Industry Association, while I fought successfully to become president of the SCHIA. I guess I always pushed for

Aleene and Gail receive trophy for best presentation of the Aleene's craftmaker paint center.

what I thought was right. Years later, I joined the board of the HIA, but I always felt that they had given crafts the short end of the stick. After a short time, many hobby shops began to have "crafts corners" in their stores, and that also helped to increase awareness and sales of the products that people like Hazel and myself were marketing. It was also through the Northern California Hobby Industry Association that I would meet Gail Eckstein, the man who was to become my second husband.

✻

Since I was very active in the Southern California Hobby Industry Association, I was invited up to San Francisco to speak to the Northern California Hobby Industry Association's annual meeting. At the time, I had a salesman in northern California who picked me up at the airport and took me to the association's meeting. I don't remember the exact nature of my presentation, but it was well-received. At the end of the night, I was going to call a cab when the president of the association introduced me to Gail Eckstein, a tall, handsome man whose family was originally of German extraction. He said he would be glad to drive me back to my hotel since it was on his way home. Gail and I ended up talking most of the night. He was an executive for a hobby model company, Western Model Distributors, and knew a lot about the hobby industry. We were both married, of course, and I had no idea that something was going to happen between us. I was taken with the fact that he knew so much about the business, and it appeared to me that we were philosophically of the same mind. We had similar views and ways of looking at the world. This first meeting was strictly professional, but I came away feeling there was something special about him, something that I found attractive.

I remember that when I tried to convince him of the value of our new line of paints and of Aleene's Tacky Glue, his response was "We don't need any more paints or glues." I said, "Sure you do." At the time, our glue was selling mainly in fibre/floral supply stores, and we were just barely making inroads into the hobby shops. I was in the process of bringing out the first spray can of soft matte paint for crafts. Nobody had come up with anything like it before we did. As far as paints were concerned, all that existed then were gloss or semi-gloss paints. I told Gail that nobody had had a soft matte paint in a spray can before, and I think that intrigued him. When I said I wanted to increase my manufacturing and sales operations, his response was, "Well, if you're going to do it, you've got to do it right." Because of his experience in the hobby-model business, he told me that if I wanted to sell to that industry certain discounts were expected. He shared other details and aspects of the business which were new to me. I think his interest in the business world must have turned me on, as well as his no-nonsense attitude about things, which was similar to mine.

In the first two months following our initial meeting, Gail and I corresponded quite a bit, focusing principally on business matters. I had to do a number of shows in Northern California, so we began seeing each other when I was up there again. It was strictly business, at least on the surface. Gail had gotten interested in helping me merchandise my

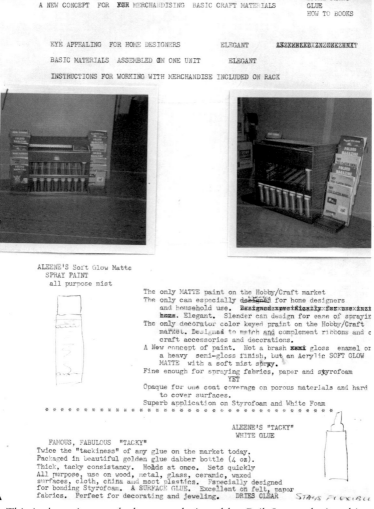

A NEW CONCEPT FOR FOR MERCHANDISING BASIC CRAFT MATERIALS   SPRAY PAINT
                                                                 GLUE
                                                                 HOW TO BOOKS

EYE APPEALING FOR HOME DESIGNERS   ELEGANT   ASZKZZBZXDXZNZWBEZHNZT

BASIC MATERIALS ASSEMBLED ON ONE UNIT   ELEGANT

INSTRUCTIONS FOR WORKING WITH MERCHANDISE INCLUDED ON RACK

ALEENE'S Soft Glow Matte
   SPRAY PAINT
      all purpose mist

The only MATTE paint on the Hobby/Craft market
The only can especially designed for home designers
  and household use. Designed especially for home
  use. Elegant. Slender can design for ease of spraying
The only decorator color keyed praint on the Hobby/Craft
  market. Designed to match and complement ribbons and c
  craft accessories and decorations.
A New concept of paint. Not a brash semi gloss enamel or
  a heavy semi-gloss finish, but an Acrylic SOFT GLOW
  MATTE with a soft mist spray.
Fine enough for spraying fabrics, paper and styrofoam
                      YET
Opaque for one coat coverage on porous materials and hard
  to cover surfaces.
Superb application on Styrofoam and White Foam

* *

                              ALEENE'S "TACKY"
                               WHITE GLUE

   FAMOUS, FABULOUS "TACKY"
Twice the "tackiness" of any glue on the market today.
Packaged in beautiful golden glue dabber bottle (4 oz).
Thick, tacky consistancy. Holds at once. Sets quickly
All purpose, use on wood, metal, glass, ceramic, waxed
surfaces, cloth, china and most plastics. Especially designed
for bonding Styrofoam. A SURFACE GLUE. Excellent on felt, paper
fabrics. Perfect for decorating and jeweling.   DRIES CLEAR   STAYS FLEXIBLE

This is the unique rack that was designed by Gail. It was during this
time of working closely with him to create a craftmakers center, that we
fell in love.

products, and he designed a rack especially for my glues and
paints, and called it a "Craftmaker Center." It was the first
one of its kind where the shelves were at an angle, so that
when you took a bottle off the rack, another one slid down
to take its place up front. We saw each other a number of
times between that September, when we first met, and

January, when there was another industry convention in Chicago. Either I was going up to the San Francisco area for demonstrations or presentations, or Gail was coming to Southern California to meet with me to discuss his ideas for helping my business. He was deeply committed to his family, and, like myself, he wasn't contemplating a divorce. Though from what he told me, Gail and his wife were living together in name only.

At the time that I met Gail and started to get interested in him, there was nothing particularly wrong with my marriage to Woody. Because of my intense business activities and my frequent traveling and presentations, it was natural for me to meet a lot of interesting men, but up until Gail, I'd never met anyone I thought I could become serious about. Woody was a very wonderful person, very nice, quiet, and certainly not demanding. I think at the time I felt I'd probably spend the rest of my life with him, but that turned out not to be the case.

With Woody, I could do anything I wanted or needed to do, go on trips, or whatever. Looking back, I see that it was good that I married him, because I didn't have any hassles at all about the professional demands I had on my time. In our business life, Woody was principally focused on our printing and art departments. And as we bought more printing equipment, he developed our printing services business. Woody heard me argue a lot with people in our business dealings, but he and I never argued at all. He was so easy-going that in all our years of marriage we'd never had a serious fight. And I never made demands on him. As I've said, Woody was very content to stay home, to be with the kids, or alone, while I was on the go all the time.

I met Gail in 1965. At the time Woody and I had been married twenty-one years. I guess I was first attracted to Gail because he was a very honest man, like Woody, and a workaholic, like myself. Both the guys I married were extremely honest, and I have to say I don't meet people like that too much any more. Both of them spoke their minds, which to me is important. I like to be able to say to someone, "I don't like you chewing gum in front of me, it annoys me." And I like to be able to have them say to me, "Well, it annoys me when you do this or that." Why annoy someone when you're with them?

They say you usually pick the same type of person the second time around, but that wasn't the case with Gail Eckstein. Honesty aside, Gail and Woody were nothing alike. Gail was an extrovert, he was out-going and liked people, liked interacting with them, while Woody preferred keeping to himself. Gail was adventurous, where Woody preferred the status quo. As president of Western Model Distributors, a leader in the model airplane field, Gail was very interested in aviation as well. And unlike Woody, who let me run the show both at home and at work, Gail had been the ruler of his home-- but this I didn't know about when we were first getting to know each other. As I would later find out, Gail had been "king" of his family, and his children were his "subjects." Truthfully, I wasn't looking for a second husband, but when I started working with Gail I found him challenging, exciting, and before too long, I realized I was in love with him.

As the months of our involvement went on, I realized that with my growing love for another man, my marriage to Woody just couldn't continue to work. I don't believe that two people are necessarily meant to be together for their entire lives. Sometimes people grow in different directions. In fact, I've seen many marriages in which people stay together and just tolerate one another, not really living, or loving, for that matter. I honestly felt that there were probably a lot of women out there who would make better wives for Woody; women who would love him and respect him, allow him the complete privacy he demanded, and be better for him than I could ever be. After our divorce, he did find a woman who was very good for him. And I never had a guilty feeling about following my heart. I was very happy that Woody found someone who would really cater to him and love him as he needed to be loved.

Gail and I could talk for hours, about business and everything else. Gail had built his own airplane, a little Whitman Tailwind, and he loved to fly. He always had goals and aspirations, like his dream to some day fly around the world in his home-built plane. After one of our meetings up north, Gail decided to drive me back to Los Angeles. I had been mulling the whole thing over and over in my mind,

Gail started building the Whitman Tailwind during his first marriage and completed it during our marriage. For several years he flew the Tailwind on business trips.

thinking about my comfortable life. By now I had five kids, four of them at home with me, and I had to decide whether or not I could or should get a divorce. On the way back to Los Angeles, we stopped at a very romantic spot called Refugio Beach, just south of Santa Ynez (where we would eventually come to live), and Gail talked to me for about an hour or two, convincing me that it would be the best thing, that we belonged together. In less than four months, we realized that we wanted to be together. At the time, I needed a manager for our business. My folks had moved on and my dad was no longer managing. I talked to Woody about it, but he was never for or against anything. And in a short time, Gail moved down to Arcadia and came to work for us. He rented an apartment nearby, and started taking additional flying lessons toward a commercial pilot's license.

Both of us had been married for about 21 years, so long that romance had faded and respect for our partners was about all that was left. A new relationship at forty-two was unbelievable. I knew divorce was going to be difficult, but seemingly so worthwhile; a chance to capture again the joy of living, loving, sharing adventures and interests with a partner. In our separate marriages, neither Gail nor I had ever contemplated divorce. Both of us had long before decided that marriage was just a comfortable state of affairs, and with all the passion gone, an acceptable situation. But when you're turned on to someone, and then when you fall in love with them, what was tolerable becomes less so.

I'm sure that Woody suspected something had come between us. He could see that I was really excited because I had someone to work with, someone who was interested in the same things, who saw the same challenges I did, and who was willing to work with me to develop our business into the manufacturing company that I had envisioned. It was after that trip, coming back from San Francisco, that I started to talk to Woody about divorce. Even then I don't think Woody took me seriously. He knew that I'd had an affair or two, but since I was never serious about anyone else and had come back to him, I'm sure he never thought I would actually divorce him. I didn't discuss my interest in Gail, though I'm sure he knew something was happening when Gail left his wife and family in the San Francisco bay area, and came to southern California to work with us.

During the fall of 1965, when all this was going on, we lived in a beautiful two-story southern colonial house in the town of Arcadia, a house we all loved and remember with such fondness. We'd moved into that house the year Tiffany was born, 1955, when it was really a two-story cracker box which we re-made over the years. First, we put a southern colonial porch on it. Then we built a large, all-purpose room out in the back, all glass with a beautiful fireplace. In those years when the kids were growing up, we entertained a lot, with people over every Friday, Saturday and Sunday. I had gotten interested in conservative politics, and so Friday nights were for political gatherings. I was very active in supporting John Rousselot for Congress, and when he won we were all elated. We became very good friends with the Rousselots, and even traveled to Washington, D.C. to visit with them. Saturdays were reserved for a dance group that met at our house every weekend, and Sunday dinners were always a gathering of one kind or another. I had done so much to that house and in that house, that to leave

This was our family's favorite home. We did a lot of entertaining, from
parties to politics, dancing, and school get togethers. The kids always
felt that this house was home.

it was really something. Getting the divorce meant selling the
house and dividing the money, and all the things that come
with splitting up. Any way you slice it, divorce is never easy.

I had four kids at home with me, Fred, Heidi, Tiffany
and Tony. My oldest daughter, Candy, had gone away to
school in Boston. I feel somewhat like I failed Candy as a
mother, in that I pushed her too hard. I thought she should
be like me, which was really dumb of me, but like all first-
time parents, I didn't know any better. Also, I just didn't
understand then that everybody is different. I think I always
felt that everyone was just like me. I just didn't realize that
there were so many different personalities in the world, and
that each one is totally unique. It's almost like each of us is
a little planet in our own orbit.

Candy was a bookworm, like her father. By the time
she was five years old, she'd read every book in the children's
library, and I had to go to bat to get her a library card in the
adult's library. Candy was quiet, and would rather read a
good book than do things I was pushing her to do. I remember I tried to force her to be interested in the things that I

thought she should be interested in, like going to dances, or just going out and doing this or that. Ultimately, I'm sure she didn't like me very much in those early years. As she was getting toward completion of high school, one of her counselors suggested she go to secretarial school, She chose Katherine Gibbs, a well-known secretarial college in Boston, in part just to get as far away from me as she could! I know this is pretty common, between some children and their parents, and I'm glad that we've been able to work it out between us over the years. Now we have a mutual admiration and respect for each other, the way it should be. Ironically, the year I was divorcing Woody to get together with Gail, Candy, at eighteen, was embarking on her own first marriage, to Peter, back east.

Gail had moved to an apartment near a house I was renting in Temple City, and had given his house up in San Leandro to his wife and kids. He gave her everything except his car and his unfinished airplane. He had an Avanti that was his pride and joy, the love of his life. He drove like a teenager. In fact he lived like a teenager. The other thing he kept after the divorce was his airplane, which was still in the process of being built. Gail's wife was so unhappy about his leaving her, that she wouldn't allow him to talk to the kids at all. He couldn't see them or talk to them for about a year, which was very upsetting to the children, and to Gail as well. Finally, they realized what their mother had done, and they were very mad at her for it. For a long time, Gail's son David didn't realize that his father wanted to contact him but didn't dare, until about two years later, when they were reunited. Later, after Gail and I were married and moved in together, his daughter, Judy, who had gotten engaged while she was going to Pepperdine College, was so angry with her mother, that she asked me to go with her to buy a wedding dress. She had the reception at our house in Arcadia, and though her mother came to the wedding, she didn't come to the reception.

Looking back on it now, I realize that I didn't even care what the children, or the rest of the family felt about the divorce. I was in love, and I didn't care. I've never had a guilty feeling about anything I've ever done, and I remember that, at the time, I really felt Woody would be better off with someone else. I gave him all the money I had. I gave him everything, knowing that he would have a harder time of it. My daughter Heidi remembers that Woody was the one who told her and the rest of the kids, that we were splitting up. Heidi screamed at him, not believing it could be true. And, in a way, that was a whole lot of people's reaction, as I recall. Woody himself, as I said earlier, was extremely surprised. We'd never fought. We'd had the freedom to pursue our own interests. So my decision to divorce was a shock to him as well as everyone else. But I knew he would meet someone who would be better for him than I was, and he did, about three years later.

*

It was really interesting how the divorce finally came about. I used my attorney in Alhambra to make arrangements for Gail and me to go to Mexico, where we could be divorced from our respective spouses, and then married, all under the same roof as it turned out. We flew down with two of the kids, Tiffany and Tony, and we landed on the American side, El Paso. Then we were collected by bus and driven over the border into Mexico.

We were brought into an attorney's office on the Mexican side of the border, and they explained to us the steps involved in getting divorced and then re-married. I remember being led into this courtyard with two guys sitting at small tables. At the first table, the divorce papers were filled out and given the official stamp of the government. You walked three steps over to the other table, and a Mexican marriage certificate was filled out and also given the official government stamp. There were about a hundred people in that courtyard, and it was one right after the other, instantly divorced, then instantly re-married. As I recall it, they read us the marriage vows in Spanish.

The reason we went to Mexico in the first place was that Gail's wife didn't want to give him a divorce. She was a very smart woman who'd been a draftsman during the war. But she never liked Gail's interest in aviation or in hobby models, because he worked hard all week, and then on weekends he'd be involved with his aviation projects and

Aleene & Gail divorced former partners and re-married in Mexico.

was rarely at home. It was in December of 1966 that we flew down and got married. But it wasn't until the following October that we were married in Pasadena, after our divorce had gone through in the U.S.

After the divorce, my oldest son, Fred, went to live with his father on a boat, a Cal 2800, then later, on a 40-foot Newporter. Fred loved to sail, and at his age, I knew he would probably be better off with his dad. After we got married, Gail and I lived together with my kids Heidi, Tiffany and Tony. We rented a house in Temple City, but we didn't stay there for long. Gail had no money because he had given everything to his wife and children, and so I decided to buy a house in Arcadia. Gail was one of those men who felt extremely responsible to his wife and children. By this time his daughter was at Pepperdine University, and his son was in his last year of high school. A year or so after we'd gotten married, when his ex-wife had loosened up about it, his son David would come down to visit us periodically, for vacations, or long weekends. Gail was trying to force David to go to an aeronautical school near where we were living, but David wanted to be a veterinarian, Gail really fought him over that. I remember that I told him I had a friend who was a vet in Southern California, and I said I'd call and maybe David could spend a couple of weeks working there-- and maybe he would see that it really wasn't for him. Well, the vet liked him so well that he offered him a job and kept him all summer! And David went on to become a very good veterinarian.

As I was soon to find out, Gail was very domineering. Even though he wasn't home a lot, when he was home,

A year later we were married in the Church of the Flowers in Pasadena,
California. We were accompanied by, from left to right Audrey Moore,
(our kids' second mother), Tiffany, Bruce (our wholesale manager),
Momma Jackson, Papa Jackson, and Tony.

he was king. Of course it wasn't easy for my kids to take
this, especially since they weren't used to that sort of thing.
Gail was the complete opposite of how Woody had been
with them. It was difficult for Gail to be with my family,
where everyone made many of their own decisions, and were
responsible for their own lives. The kids had jobs to do, but
they were really quite "free." I was busy working. And with
Audrey, my dependable housekeeper and their "second
mother," my kids had a freedom which was, perhaps, unusual. Certainly it was quite the opposite of Gail's family scene.

Our home was open to all of my childrens' friends. I
remember one neighbor who couldn't wait to get rid of her
kids, to send them over to our house, and get them out of her
hair. Our home became the gathering place for the entire
neighborhood. We had rules that the children knew they had
to follow; jobs that had to be done; lawns to be mowed, that
kind of thing, before they could engage in their activities. I
was the boss of the house, the one who meted out the warn-

ings, and I wasn't adverse to a spanking if needed, but the need seldom arose. I always told my children that if they got into trouble, or were with friends who'd gotten into trouble, they need not worry about the police, because when I got hold of them, they would get something they'd never forget! Fortunately, they all believed me, so things never got to that point.

But Gail's attempt to bring his "absolute ruler" attitude into our newly blended family wasn't going to work. Tiffany had gotten into it with Gail because he insisted she cook dinner several times during the week. She didn't want to, and she wasn't about to be bossed around. I think it was during the Crafts Caravan, that Tiffany moved out. She was only seventeen then, but she knew what she wanted and what she didn't. Tony, who was only five when Gail and I got together, suffered more at first. Gail was really hard on him, very demanding, probably as Gail's own father had been on him. But Gail also taught Tony a lot about fixing electrical problems, about plumbing, and lots of other basic skills. As a result, Tony can fix anything, and make anything. He's just really talented that way. Of course, Woody also was that way. He could do anything with his hands, and I'm sure it was passed on genetically to the kids. But overall, Gail was really rough with the kids. This caused a strain in me, between the two sides, which I never got used to.

CHAPTER FIVE

The Craftmakers Caravan

The Craftmaker's Caravan was credited with being the "start" of the Craft Industry and I was given credit for being the pioneer in the Industry. I don't know what inspired me to come up with the idea for a Craftmakers Caravan, but like most good ideas, it was the follow-through that made it a great success, both for us and for the crafts industry as a whole. It was in the fall of 1967 that the idea for a nationwide caravan first hit me: it would be a way to educate the public on what crafts were all about. Immediately, I started to plan it out.

At first, I think I was only going to do it in a small way. But when Hazel and her company, Hazel Pearson Handicrafts, and Carl "Gus" Gustafsson, owner of Natcol Plastics, wanted to join with me, I expanded the idea to include some 33 major cities over a period of six months. As a result, we exposed many thousands, if not hundreds of thousands, of people to crafts.

Gus had a business in liquid plastic resins. He'd take Christmas ornaments and pour the liquid plastic resin into them. When the resin set, he would break off the ornament and be left with a beautiful grape cluster or other shapes which could be used in decorations. You'd get a branch with his package, and you could make a wonderful grape cluster to set on your table. Hazel Pearson, who was to become one of my best friends, was teaching crafts and just getting her own business off the ground at the same time I was.

At the time, I was doing classes for dealers at my shop on Sundays. In order to offer a variety of crafts, I asked Hazel to participate by showing what she was working on. At her suggestion, I invited Gus one Sunday to join us. Remember, store owners worked six days a week then, with

Over 20,000 people, 5 deep, around the block, waiting to get into our first Craftmaker Caravan Show in Pasadena, California.

Sunday being their only free day off. But they came anyway, and they loved what we were offering.

For six months, from January to June, 1968, we traveled across the country, demonstrating crafts, teaching "how-to," and showing the materials. Our largest show, which was the first one of the caravan, was held in Pasadena, California, and brought in over 20,000 people! I think the smallest number we ever had was around 5,000, a huge success by any standards. After Pasadena, we went on to San Francisco, and then Seattle, then Phoenix, Dallas, San Antonio, Houston, St. Louis, Atlanta, and Virginia Beach, Va. We continued on to Boston, Detroit, Chicago, Cleveland and Denver. Six months later, after forty-nine shows in as many cities, we were at our last stop, Salt Lake City, Utah.

Our traveling craftmakers' roadshow was held in metropolitan areas where there were hobby model distributors and retailers, or even individual craftspeople who could help us produce the show. We contacted the local people in advance and they would go out and find the building for us to rent, usually a convention center, a county fair building, a mall, or even a hotel somewhere with at least 5,000 square feet of meeting space. They would also help me by placing publicity stories and ads in the newspaper in advance of the event. The local contact would get dealers or interested retailers involved with our show, invite community leaders from the Girl Scouts and other organizations, such as parks & recreation departments, anyone and everyone who was interested in crafts in their city. I had a whole outline of the tasks involved for the contact to follow, all geared toward making a success of the show.

At the time, I was doing a lot of television, and it was easy for me to get bookings in advance of our appearances. I would contact either the news departments, or the "Women's Page" editors of TV stations, newspapers and radio stations, and it wasn't unusual for me to be on three or four different shows in one city a day or so before our scheduled events. Usually I did five-minute segments showing the kinds of things that they would see demonstrated at our event the next day.

Our first show in Pasadena (where there was a line around the block five people deep!) made me realize we had

FAMOUS CRAFT DESIGNER TO APPEAR IN PERSON AT CRAFTMAKERS FAIR

Aleene, famous Craft authority and television personality will be appearing, in person, in this area at the unique Creative Craftmakers Fair that will be held on _____ at the _____. Aleene, appeared as a regular on the Tennessee Ernie Ford program and with Gypsy Rose Lee, produced and mc'd her own Hobby and Craft Television Show for many years and has lectured throughout the United States on Arts and Crafts. Currently she is appearing weekly on the FYI Tom Frandsen Show on NBC-TV Channel 4, and will appear locally on the _____. Appearing at the Craftmakers show, she will feature several presentations and demonstrations on the newest craft products and newest craft techniques.

Aleene and her husband Mr. Gail Eckstein publish a library of Craft "how to" books including Projects from Tissue Paper, Feather Flowers, how to make flowers and novelties from ribbon, felt, foil, styrofoam, chenille, and velour. In addition Aleene is the foremost authority on "working with junk". Over half of her publications feature the use of discrads such as egg cartons, old containers, macaroni, plastic bleach bottles, mach'ing with newspaper and hundreds of other throwaways. She shows how you can take the junk and transform it into beautiful decorations, novelties, designs, displays and gifts. One of the features of her presentation now is making flowers from bread.

Aleene shows how easy it is to create useful and decorative items. "Everyone can be Creative, everyone can be a Craftmaker, all you need to know are a few basic procedures and you will be able to produce beautiful professional designs for your home, your family, your friends. You can make additional money by selling your crafts, or you can save money by creating all of your gifts."

You are invited to attend the free demonstration and exhibit and to meet Aleene, at the Creative Craftmakers Fair. Free tickets are available at your local Hobby and Craft stores.

For further information:

Publicity for the Craftmaker Caravan was given to hobby distributors, dealers, and crafters to put into their local newspapers.

I did a 45 minute demo every hour in a special presentation area.
The show was open 9:00-12:00, 1:00-4:00 and 7:00-9:00.

There were two other presentation areas with hourly demos featuring Hazel and Natcol demonstrators.

a winner on our hands, and we hadn't even gotten out on the road yet! Entrance to all our shows was free. The layout of that event became the format for the rest of our shows around the country. In three corners of the hall, I set up stage areas, and every hour we'd put on a thirty-minute demonstration for the audiences. Hazel's people had one of the stages, Gus' another, and I had the third.

At our table locations, I set up large boards with samples of the made-up crafts that matched the instruction books we were selling, so people could see what the finished product would look like. And I had everything packed perfectly in great big boxes, so the whole thing could be broken down and quickly loaded onto the truck, and back on the road to the next city. Two guys from Natcol drove the truck, while Hazel and her people were in a large, camper-type van. Since I was doing a lot of television, I would fly in to the next city in advance, appear on TV, do some promotion, then do the show, and then fly home for a couple of days to the FYI Show in Los Angeles. Then I would fly back out to the next Caravan show, often bringing one or more of the kids with me.

At the shows, I demonstrated a number of different things you could make, but I only sold our how-to books, since it would have been a conflict with hobby-model retailers in those cities who were selling our products themselves. But I knew that if the people bought our books on how to make different crafts, they would then go out and buy the materials from their local retailers. Gus' guys were demonstrating their liquid plastic resins, and Hazel's people at their tables were showing all the things that she had been developing. But as we'd agreed, the three of us only sold instruction books, not the products themselves. We didn't want to take the business away from local retailers and distributors.

We were lucky that Pasadena was our first event, because it was close to home, and when we ran out of materials we could run over to our warehouse in Temple City to get more boxes of instruction sheets. At the time, Aleene's published over 100 books on everything from working with gold leafing, to paper mache, to working with ribbons, tissue paper flowers, and everything in between that we thought people would want to make. We were so crowded

Our Craftmaker Caravan was financed by the sales of Aleene, Hazel and Natcol books.
Note: panels holding designs from books.

Every hour we had a prize drawing. Above, people on stage and projects featured on display panels.

In order to have lots of activity in the show, I had 10-20 tables to which we invited guests to sit down at no charge and make a small project. I was the first to call this "MAKE-IT AND TAKE-IT."

Our view from the stage was pretty exciting to see. Thousands of enthusiastic crafters came to see what we had to present.

and so busy at that Pasadena show, that I had to shanghai
people I knew to help us out with the booths and with collecting money! But once Pasadena was a great success, we
sent pictures ahead to the cities on our route, and it got us
really good media attention in advance of our arrival.

Each show had set hours: 9 -12 noon, 1-4 p.m., and
7-9 p.m. When you came into the auditorium you could get
a free ticket to participate at a "Make It & Take It" table, a
phrase I originally coined for the Craft Caravan. I wanted an
activity going on at the show where people could come and
make something to take home with them. We supplied the
materials for free, and gave the audience a place where they
could sit down and actually make a craft item according to
our instructions. The ticket gave them a time at a specific
table to make the particular craft they chose. This is the kind
of thing that's great promotion, and also gives the customers
a chance to really work with the products.

People would browse through the whole auditorium,
stopping at those tables or displays which caught their interest. In the bookstore, we had wooden display boards with
finished crafts next to a copy of the instruction book for that
particular item. We also did demonstrations on how to do
the different crafts. At the time, I was still showing
Formosan Wood Flowers, Aleene's Tacky Glue, tissue paper
flowers and things like that. And I was teaching Bread
Dough Flower-making. I'd take a slice of bread, and a table-
spoon of my Aleene's Tacky Glue, and mix it into a dough,
and then make flowers from it. I had Fred, Heidi and Tiffany
come with me to many of the shows. Tony, who was then
about eight years old, also did a number of the shows, and
believe it or not, at eight years old he'd be teaching people
how to make Bread Dough Flowers! Every hour we'd have
a prize drawing, and Tony would get up on the stage and
announce the winner. He was always busy, always working,
and from these experiences he learned early on how to deal
with the public, as have all my kids.

The Craft Caravan really jump-started the whole
craft industry. As I've said earlier, up until that time there
was no clearly-defined industry, no association, and no
crafts stores, they just didn't exist. Our products were beginning to show up in hobby shops, and a few department

Hazel, Jim Gick, Frank's wife and Frank. Frank was in charge of Hazel's demos. Frank's wife was in charge of make-it and take-it tables.

stores, but after the Craft Caravan, there was a sprouting of crafts stores in many of the cities we'd visited, and many of the craftpeople we met started serving as dealers and distributors in their areas.

Up until the Crafts Caravan, I'd been selling my products directly to wood fibre retail shops, and mostly in California. With Gail's help, and our new "Craft Center" racks, I was starting to make inroads to the hobby model shops, but just barely. Remember, I began as a small retail store, then became a distributor as I sold to other retail stores, and then, as a result of the Caravan, I became a manufacturer selling to distributors who in turn sold to stores. Prior to that, I'd had a couple of large chains, like Frank's Nursery, who usually bought a lot of craftmaking materials near Christmas to add to their holiday season sales, and who also ended up helping me with the Craft Caravan. But with six months of very well-attended shows all around the country, I had proven to the hobby model shops that larger and larger numbers of people were interested in crafts, and that they could have successful crafts sections in their stores. In the months following the caravan, my sales increased substantially.

I remember one lady, in particular, Marjorie Suzinski from Philadelphia. She was an enthusiastic crafts person who wanted to become a distributor, and she promoted crafts throughout her area. There was also a lady in Milwaukee who set up parties in her home to demonstrate our products, and she also became a distributor for us. So it was a people-to-people kind of thing, the way our company grew, and in good measure as a result of the Craft Caravan. It got a little complicated, of course, because there were no crafts distributors, per se, and the hobby model industry had its own set of rules when it came to territories and distributorships. But we were creating a new industry and there really weren't any rules for it yet. Gail, whose hobby model company had been one of the founders of the Hobby Industry Association (HIA), didn't want us to break any of their rules, even though crafts was a field of its own. The hobby model field had a set structure, involving retailer, distributor and manufacturer. Gail couldn't understand that because it was so new, the crafts field wasn't similarly structured. Someone who had a little craft shop and wanted to become a distributor was usually very gung-ho to promote crafts. But Gail made a number of people mad when he said he wouldn't sell to them as distributors. Ironically, a few of them grew to be our biggest customers. But things were changing and I could see that it wasn't going to hurt anyone to start some outlets in different places, though I still had to be careful not to step on anyone's toes.

It's a funny thing, but about twenty-five years ago, right around 1970, the crafts industry completely overtook the hobby model business. When I was first getting into it, hobby models were the thing. Slowly but surely though, crafts began to grow and grow and grow. It was one of those slow-changing things you don't really notice, but more and more craft people started joining the HIA. Today, as I write this, the Hobby Industry Association is probably 99% crafts!

There was a time when I fought fiercely to have the name of association changed to reflect this change, but the industry never acknowledged that it's now a crafts industry.

This sort of annoyed me for a long time. First, I thought the name should be something like Hobby & Crafts Association, but they argued that the word "hobby" included crafts by definition, I replied, "no, hobbies are stamp collecting, model railroads, airplane models, stuff like that." But at the time that I was trying to change the name, most of the people voting were hobby model people who didn't want to change it. I felt that for publicity purposes, such as when the industry association would send out press releases, we needed to have the word "craft" in there somewhere. After a while the crafts industry grew to be so large, I sort of gave up fighting for it.

It was also around that time that the first real crafts magazine called *Profitable Crafts*, was being launched, by an acquaintance of mine, Jack Wax. There were hobby model publications up until then, but Jack was the first one to come up with a magazine specifically for our field. Hazel Pearson and I were really instrumental in getting him started, as we shared all the names of people we knew who would buy

Hazel and Aleene today, 1996. Hazel is now retired but active in teaching crafts at her Church. Hazel should be remembered as one of the craft industry pioneers.

space in his magazines. He in turn helped publicize what we were all about. By the time the Craft Caravan came to a conclusion in June of '68, the crafts field had emerged as an industry of its own, one which would grow to be the multi-billion dollar-a-year-business it is today.

*

When we finished the Craft Caravan, I immediately flew down to Guadalajara, Mexico, with Gail, Tony and Tiffany, as a hostess on a craft tour and then went on a "working" cruise back from Mexico to California. I'd set this up with a travel agency. My family and I would teach crafts on board the cruise ship, in exchange for which we got free trips. We toured the Tlaquepaque, Guadalajara's open-air crafts market, then San Miguel de Allende, an artistic American colony which had incredible paper mache objects, Mexico City, and then went on to Acapulco. There we boarded the S.S. Princess, which I think was on its maiden voyage. We met a lot of really nice folks on that trip, but I was exhausted from six months of flying back and forth to the Craft Caravan. By the time we docked in Los Angeles I was ready to get home!

Home at that time was no picnic either. Gail wasn't the easiest person to get along with. He was so different from Woody, whom I'd gotten used to after twenty-one years of marriage. I'd been so free, and very much in charge during my marriage to Woody, but marriage to Gail was another story. There were clashes, as I recall, about business and about family as well. Don't get me wrong-- Gail was a very nice person, and like Woody, 100% honest. He was extremely well-liked in the hobby and crafts industry, as well as in the aviation field. We had good times and bad as in all marriages.But overall, I feel I've had two very good husbands, for which I'm grateful. Oddly enough, I got married at 21, and both my marriages were almost exactly 21 years in duration.

By this time, as I've said, my oldest daughter Candy had completed school in Boston, and had just gotten married to her first husband, Peter. Fred had gone to live with his father. Though he visited us a lot, he wasn't living with Gail and me. Heidi was very busy with her boyfriend, Jimmy, whom she would soon marry, so she was almost out the door herself; which really left Tiffany, about fourteen at the time, and Tony, about nine, at home with us.

Gail was really rough on the kids, and I have to assume that it had a lot to do with how he was brought up. Where Woody had been gentle, Gail was not, especially with Tony. In my first marriage, if there was any spanking to be done, I did it. But with Gail, it was a different story. He demanded to be the disciplinarian, and we fought about it quite often. During the Craft Caravan, I had to fly Tiffany out to wherever we were on numerous occasions, because she and Gail were fighting so much. But somehow, Gail never seemed to understand that these kids didn't want to be bossed around. I guess he thought it was his duty as a man, or as a step-father, to behave that way, though I'm sure it has a lot to do with his own early conditioning.

Gail also didn't like the way I favored Tony, my youngest son. He always felt I was too nice to Tony; that I did too much for him, and that I treated him differently than the other kids, which, I suppose, to some extent, I did. In a way, I always felt like Tony and I spoke the same language. Tony had the same spark and interests that I had. I liked working with him, which I think somehow also got to Gail. In spite of Gail's' need to be a disciplinarian, my kids really didn't need too much discipline. They were all hard workers from childhood on. They were ringing the cash register while standing on a stepstool when they were very small, from about five years on up. And they were always helping out in other ways, too, like packaging and labeling. Anything that they could do at the shop, they did.

Even though I had Audrey, our housekeeper who was with us for seventeen years, she wasn't there on Saturdays and Sundays. If I had to go to the supermarket, that's where the kids went. I took them with me just about everywhere. When I went on trips, teaching classes or what-ever, I took them with me. So, in that way, they were always in and around my business, every one of them, including Candy, right from their childhoods. Of course when she got old enough to get a job, because of the friction between us, Candy went to work for a dress shop. Each one of my children went off on their own a bit, as kids want and need to do. But over time, they worked many shows with me, not just the Craft Caravan. They traveled a lot and grew up in the business. As much as possible, I emphasized, that ours was a family business, because family is and has been so important to me in my life.

I was also of the mind that traveling, for the kids, was as beneficial, if not more so, than school. Today, schools probably wouldn't allow parents to take their kids on as many trips as I took mine on, which I think is too bad. In fact, after we moved up to Santa Ynez, and Tony was in ninth or tenth grade, one of his teachers asked the class what states or foreign countries they'd visited. When Tony started reeling off the different places he'd been, the teacher thought he was being naughty and making it up, until she realized it was all true.

A little further on in this book, you'll find my kids telling some of their anecdotes and their version of family stories. I know their remembrances are a lot different from mine. I'm sure they'll recall that every meal was "creamed tuna on toast," since I was such a lousy cook. Yet Audrey cooked five days a week for them and was an excellent cook, in addition to being their "second mother." While I didn't cook much, on the weekends as a rule I would go to my local market and come home with pre-cooked roasts, making sure we always had a full refrigerator. But all they remember is creamed tuna on toast!

Speaking of kids, one of the reasons I'm writing this book, I suppose, is that one of my biggest regrets in life is that I never stopped and talked to my great-grandmother, to learn some of the details of her life. She'd traveled in a covered wagon from Iowa up to South Dakota. Once there, she was attacked by Indians, then rescued by the man who would become her husband. She lived with us, up into her nineties, but I still never asked her anything about her life. I know very little about either of my grandparents. Now I'm really unhappy that I never talked to them about their lives. I just vaguely know the stories of my parents' lives. It's really one of the curious mysteries of life, how we know so little about our parents or grandparents lives, let alone that of our great-grandparents, and yet we're here because of them, because of everyone who came before us. In a way, when my daughter Tiffany asked me why I was writing this book, I realized that's one of the reasons.

Parenting is another one of those mysteries. They don't give you a manual or "how-to" instructions when your kids are born. Each of us naturally does it in her or his own way. Of course, to a great extreme, the way we raise our kids is a result of how we, ourselves, were brought up. We tend to repeat some of the patterns we learned from our parents, consciously or unconsciously, both the good and the bad. I know that because I grew up with a lot of freedom and independence and I gave the same to my kids. Woody, because he chose to be a removed kind of a guy, also gave our kids that sense of independence. But life with Gail was another matter.

With more and more "Craft Centers" being set-up in retail outlets around the country, my business grew. Like most businesses that are growing, costs and overhead increase when you're expanding. My books and instruction sheets were selling well, and I'd started sending them out to a printer who had a big web press and was able to do more than what our press could do. Sales of Aleene's Tacky Glue and my line of paints were increasing, and the orders poured in during the months after the Crafts Caravan. We had about 70 employees at the time, and that also affected the expansion of the costs of our operations.

In addition to our published crafts designs and instructions, I had two versions of a monthly newsletter called "The Petal Pusher," one for our dealers and one for consumers. Each month I'd also give them new marketing ideas in the form of instruction sheets and books. We published a catalogue, thick with pages and pages of products we were offering. I remember that at Christmas we did Tissue Paper Wreaths, Deco Foil Angels, and Chenille Bump Christmas Tree Corsages. For Easter, we offered things like Feather Easter Lilies, a Bunny Bowl, and an assortment of ducks-- using Styrofoam® shapes, of course. We offered information on all kinds of floral and holiday decorations that anyone could make. And each flower in our instruction sheets took something different. A delphinium, for example, took covered wire for the stem, florist tape to wrap the stem wire, stamens, leaves, and the wood fiber which came in different colors. I was always coming up with new products and ways to package and market ideas.

Speaking of marketing, I had originally been buying my spray paint from a company called Illinois Bronze. Everything was going okay at first, but when I started selling more and more to a particular customer, Illinois Bronze stepped in and tried to take over that account themselves. I remember I argued with them that they couldn't do that, but they said they could. As a result, I took all the paint that I had on hand and flooded the market with it at a cheap price. I was pretty angry about them trying to take away my customers, and it led me into developing my own line of paints with my own label. You see, there are very few people who actually manufacture paint. Most companies get their supply from about five or six major paint people. That's just the way it is. It doesn't matter how much you can sell; you can't sell enough to make it worthwhile to grind your own pigments. But when I started bottling it in spray cans with my own Aleenc's label, my sales started to shoot up.

During this time, Gail was managing the company for me, and while he did a good job, naturally we had our problems. For one thing, I was a risk-taker, and he was just the opposite. Taking risks is a big part of business, just as it is a part of our lives. You have to take the risks, but carefully. I don't go all out on something. I try to keep tight control over what I'm doing, so that I can limit my losses if they should occur. But it's not enough to have a good idea, or even a good intuitive feeling about something. If a "good idea" ends up costing you too much money so that it becomes a loss, then it wasn't such a good idea after all. But yes, take the risk when it's appropriate, when it holds the promise of success, and when your intuition is telling you to. If you don't, you'll never get anywhere. I remember a quote I heard once about that, something like "You can't discover new oceans unless you have the courage to lose sight of the shore." I think it's that simple.

But I'm also talking about developing your intuition, a gift which I believe we're all born with, but which too few choose to develop. Just a couple of days ago, I was over at our television studio when someone came in with a brand new product. There were a few of us present when the man was demonstrating. I took one look and went bananas over it. Immediately, I could see, or intuit, the possibilities.

I always keep my eyes open for the potential of a product or a situation. I like to try and think how someone else could make good use of it. Just to see the product used like a cake-decorating tube didn't impress me too much. But when it was painted and antiqued, it was gorgeous! It turned a not-very attractive table into something that looked very fine and expensive. So having a developed sense of intuition, and using it, seems to me to be the difference between who succeeds and who doesn't. You can refine your intuition, like any skill or talent, but you have to practice using it, listening to it, in order to develop it. I like to act on my intuition, and even the few times that it could be called "wrong," in another sense of the word it usually turned out to be "right." This was something that I think Gail never really understood about me, or appreciated.

Another thing had to do with money. Gail always had a problem around money, a kind of insecurity, that it wouldn't be there for him when he needed it. I had just the opposite feeling. Money always seemed to appear for me. It was such a laugh with Gail, sometimes, because there'd be some money problems, and I'd say, don't worry, everything's fine, and the next day money would appear. And sometimes it came from the strangest places, out of the blue, in the mail, or when I least expected it, but certainly could use it! Also, I was very much a "saver," money-wise. I always kept putting money away. It's funny about money. Because everyone always thought I had a lot of it when I didn't, but regardless, I always seemed to be able to do what I wanted.

When Woody and the family moved to our two-story house, everyone thought we were millionaires, and we weren't. We always had a new car, and we always lived well, because everything I did kept increasing. When I bought that two-story crackerbox house for $30,000 (back in the dark ages of the 1960s!), I later sold it for double the original price. Then, when Gail and I married, I bought a place for $40,000 and sold it for $75,000 a few years later. I know I've had good luck with property and real estate, but I also know that it has to do with more than luck-yes, it's intuition.

I think another serious difference between Gail and myself had to do with change. Dr. Ernest Holmes, the founder of the Church of Religious Science, said "Change is the only constant in the universe," and that has always stuck with me. I've welcomed change, embraced it, really, and I know this was another thing about me that Gail never really understood.

A little later on in this book, I'm going to have a chapter on my philosophy about life, but I'd like to share some thoughts here with you. These have been compiled by my oldest daughter, Candy Liccione, who lives in Pennsylvania and is very involved in raising herbs. It's funny, but inspite of all the friction and complications of our early years together as mother and daughter, a lot of her thoughts presented here are very close to my own. I try to remember and act on these as I go through my very busy day. And I'm still working on a number of them, too. Maybe some of these ideas will ring your bell as well:

- Be willing to drop rigid beliefs.
- Give up harsh judgments about fellow humans.
- Don't be ruled by judgments.
- Change your mind whenever you please.
- Think, question, philosophize.
- Realize how impressive peace is.
- Don't run on a strict time schedule. Slow down and allow room for something interesting to develop.
- Have a flexible mind and body.
- Make an ass out of yourself once in a while. It can do you good.
- Never "live down" to anyone's expectations.
- Be a good friend to yourself.
- Be authentic.
- Dare to be humorous. Dare to be yourself.
- Allow space for imperfection in yourself and

others. Our imperfections make us interesting.

- Let go of your gripes. Surrender your stubborn ways.
- Don't let yourself think or feel that you are at the mercy of the world. God's angels are guarding you day and night.
- Pay attention to your gut feelings.
- Try something new often.
- Give up any defensive attitude you may carry around. It's okay to make mistakes or to be "wrong."
- Breathe deeply at least once an hour.
- Let yourself feel enthusiastic about something, anything.
- Know you deserve the best that the angels have to offer.
- Explore, experiment, enjoy things. Expect the unexpected, and leave window open for a spirit.
- Cultivate laughing attacks, and think of something wild to do each day, so as to keep your Guardian Angel well entertained and happy.
- Let Freedom Ring!

*

One more thing, I don't know about you, but I'm an inveterate "clipper outer" of magazines and newspapers. Anything that strikes my imagination, or captures my attention, I like to tear out and save for later reflection. I recently clipped the following item from an announcement of the Santa Barbara Unity Church, which exactly reflected my own feelings and which I'd like to share with you:

"Every person, to some degree, makes his own age. I have a friend who is 77, and he goes from morning until night, never seeming to get tired. He is too busy expressing life to think about getting old. There are others who talk constantly about their fear of advancing years, and they indulge in self-pity, and thus speed up the aging process. Much depends on keeping our interest high in life and in developing new interests. Remember that, how old you are, depends on how interested you are in everything that goes on around you. You are eternally alive in God."

A publicity picture of Aleene and Hazel for the Craftmaker Caravan
Show, which featured roughly 150 books that were for sale.

Aleene holding the HIA Trophy for the best booth design, at the introduction of Aleene's new Spray paint and craftmaker center.

CHAPTER SIX

The Dangers of Success

It was in July of 1969, that Aleene's, Inc., became the first crafts-related company in our industry to be acquired by a larger entity, Aurora, Inc. It looked like a step in the right direction for us, but turned out to be a "disaster," in several senses of the word. But, as usual, it was a positive learning experience for me.

At the time, we were growing too fast, and it's not easy to finance a business that is growing too fast. In the wake of the popularity of the Craft Caravan, as well as my ongoing efforts on television, our sales were increasing but so was our overhead. Gail didn't like it at all. It made him nervous. As I've said before, he didn't like owing money, and when you grow, you owe, at least for a time. It's one of the realities of business life. In fact, Gail's anxieties were probably the primary reason I decided to accept an offer from Aurora to buy out Aleene's Inc.

I don't know whether it was Gail who brought up the idea of selling to someone else or myself, but I recall that we were fighting about money, when several people approached me, saying they wanted to buy me out. One represented a company called Craftmaster, a paint-by-the-numbers company that was doing extremely well at the time. And then came Aurora, with it's model railroads and model racing cars, that kind of stuff.

According to what they told me, they were gung-ho to have a craft division. It so happened that Gail and I knew the people from Aurora and we liked them. I thought it was a great opportunity. Of course, I was wrong, and it was a disaster from day one. I've often said that the sale should "never have happened," but in the final analysis, it was a good change, because it gave me the freedom to try several new things that I never would've gotten to, like candle crafting, painting, stitchery, and other interests I was able to explore during the year or so that we were owned by someone else.

At the time, Aurora was one of the leading companies in the model car and airplane field. They were going great guns, with plants everywhere in Holland, England, France, and a number of other countries. The two top executives who'd come to discuss it with us said they were very impressed with our company, and what we'd been able to do in expanding and promoting the crafts industry. They believed that with additional promotion and publicity, Aurora could turn me into the "Betty Crocker" of the crafts world. Unfortunately, fairly soon after we were bought out by them, these same executives left the company, and a totally different set of people was put in charge of Aleene's, Inc., now a division of Aurora. It wasn't that the new people were "bad" or anything, they were just stupid about the crafts

During the "disaster" I worked with Tom Yaley, of Yaley Ent., to design, package, promote and sell his line of candle crafting materials.

July 1, 1969

CRAFT AND FLORAL SUPPLIES

P. O. BOX A   *   9119 EAST LAS TUNAS DRIVE   *   TEMPLE CITY, CALIFORNIA 91780

AREA CODE 213 -   287-6147   -   283-6247

Good Morning

Exciting things are happening here at Aleene's. We have just completed arrangements transferring the stock of our company to Aurora Plastics Corp., a leading Hobby manufacturer. Aurora's management, in reviewing their product line recognized the need for girls and women's hobbies. The logical answer in this product area is CRAFTS. And when talking about crafts, it's Aleene's, naturally.

Aurora's entry into the Craft field in this way proves their interest in this expanding business, they will more closely tie the hobby and craft field together and will set the stage for more growth and more and more volume for the whole industry.

We are involved in big, big plans for the future. The first most noticeable change will be an improvement in our merchandise availability. Fewer back orders will help both of us. Secondly, new products that we would have liked to add to improve our line will now be a possibility. Third, the Aurora sales people contacting you will now be writing orders for our merchandise freeing Aleene for more designs and promotional efforts.

There will be no change in our merchandising. We will continue working with our Distributor-Customers, hopefully adding a few new ones to fill in some gaps.

Our order desk, production, and shipping facilities will be moved to Downey, Calif. Aleene will remain in Temple City with our Design Staff. I will be operating out of Downey keeping you up to date and maintaining our contact through the Aurora salesmen.

Aleene and I both want to thank you for your support and cooperation in the past and look forward to both a pleasant and more profitable relationship in the future.

Sincerely,

Vice President
Aleene's Incorporated

On behalf of Aurora's management we are pleased to have become part of the vital craft field through our association with Aleene's. We welcome the customers, suppliers and friends of Aleene to the Aurora family and look forward to the continuation and strengthening of prior relationships.

Very truly yours,
AURORA WEST

Herbert L. Raff
General Manager

NEW ADDRESS: ALEENE'S
12152 Woodruff Ave.
Downey, Calif. 90241

NEW PHONE: A/C 213 923-5493

CRAFTMAKER PRODUCTS

* CRAFTMAKER CENTERS   * ALEENE'S MATTE SPRAY PAINT   * ALEENE'S TACKY WHITE GLUE   * ALEENE'S HOW TO CRAFT BOOKS
ALEENE'S CRAFT BOOK CAROUSEL * CRAFTMAKER TISSUE PAPER   * CRAFTMAKER VELOUR CREPE PAPER   * CRAFTMAKER ANTIQUING DIP
* CRAFTMAKER GLAZE   * CRAFTMAKER CHENILLE STEMS   * CRAFTMAKER DREAM PUFF * CRAFTMAKER FEATHERS * CRAFTMAKER DECO FOIL

business. I realized fairly soon after the ink was dry on the contract that I shouldn't have allowed my company to be bought out, but I was a little too late. They just didn't know what they were doing, and all their expansive talk about how they were going to develop and expand the company turned out to be just that, talk.

In our original agreement, I was to be a public relations and promotion consultant for Aleene's, Inc., now a division of Aurora, while Gail stayed on as a manager/consultant. But it didn't work out the way it was planned. As a world-wide company, Aurora had the resources to expand Aleene's, Inc., to develop new ideas and new products, and to market us in ways that we never could, due to lack of the kind of money required to expand. At least, that's how it looked on paper, on the contract we all signed. But the disastrous part of it was that they just didn't know what they were doing. In the fourteen months that they owned us, they just about killed the company. For me personally, it was like they were killing my baby.

For one thing, within three months after Aurora took over, they changed the formulation of Aleene's Tacky Glue! Aurora thought I was paying too much money for it, so Aurora started buying from a different manufacturer with a different formula, just because they got a better overall price. Aurora's executives reasoned that "none of the customers will know the difference." Boy were they wrong! They had absolutely no idea that the glue I used was really good, really special. So they went ahead and changed it. (It was then, by the way, that my dad went right down to Borden and got the rights to my original formulation, and started putting it up under Heidi's name, as Heidi's Tacky Glue. That way the rights to the original tacky glue stayed in the family. Our retail operation wasn't on their agenda, so it was turned over to my daughter Heidi, who ran the store in conjunction with Grandpa and Grandma Jackson.)

Another mistake that Aurora made which upset me no end, was that they changed our bottle from gold, which everyone knew and was familiar with, to a white bottle with purple printing on it. Everyone in the crafts field knew my gold bottle because it was such a distinctive identifier. But to the experts in New York, that apparently didn't matter much. They even went so far as to change the name to Aleene's Mighty Tacky Glue. Meanwhile, people like Hazel, who'd never come up against me, came out with Hazel's Tacky Glue, and about ten others followed suit. As it turned out, we couldn't copyright the words "tacky glue" because they were a descriptive phrase, so all I could copyright was "Aleene's Tacky Glue." In the interim, during the time Aurora owned our company, it seemed like everyone else in the crafts business came out with their own versions of "tacky glue." And when I got the company back later, I had to fight all those competitors, separate from the other problems of starting over for a second time.

In addition to buying out our stock in Aleene's, Inc., and also buying out my ex-husband's shares, Aurora had us under contract as consultants, though communications from them were few and far between. They just weren't interested in taking advantage of what we had to offer. They brought in specialists, experts from companies such as Revlon, which was part of their group, and Ideal Toy Co., but they had very little to do with me at all. They asked me to come to the January 1970 HIA show, and to be present in their Aleene's, Inc., booth. I went because I had to under the terms of the contract, but I sure didn't feel like being there. This was after they'd changed both the formulation and the color of the bottle. In a way, it was almost too much for me to bear. I remember that I stood right at the edge of the booth at that HIA show and chit-chatted with people as they came by, but that was about all I did. As far as they were concerned, I was just an appendage to their operation of Aleene's, Inc., and that left me both frustrated and angry at the same time.

*

While they had the company, I hardly had anything to do with it. They thought their New York people knew a lot more than I did about the crafts industry, so I was really cut loose to do anything I pleased. During that period, when it became clear to me that they weren't too interested in what I had to offer, I put my attention elsewhere. I took some courses in stitchery and painting, things I'd always wanted to learn. That's why I've always said that even though it seemed like a "disaster" at the time, and everyone in the industry treated it as a disaster, it gave me the freedom to look into other things that I'd never had the time for, and which I started to develop for future use.

About six months after Aurora officially bought us in July 1969, when it was good and obvious that they didn't want my active participation, I decided to take a trip to Ireland. I had a kind of carte blanche agreement with Aurora that I could develop promotional ideas and research new products, and it was my opinion that going to Ireland should be part of the research. I let them know my plans in advance, informing them that I would be charging the trip to the company since it was for research purposes. When I didn't hear a word back from them, I decided that they obviously had no objections, and so off we went.

I remember contacting the Irish government in advance of our trip, and telling them that I wanted to do a craft-related tour of Ireland. I told them that I'd be putting some of it on television in the U.S. upon my return, since I

Our craft tour of Ireland - in a "gypsy tinker's wagon," Aleene, Gail, Tiffany and Tony.

was doing a lot of TV at the time. We were able to connect with the right people over there who, in turn, pointed the way and introduced us to craftspeople in Ireland.

As I recall, I'd first gotten interested in the idea when I'd read in the *National Geographic* magazine about caravans going through County Cork. Gail, Tony, and Tiffany went with me, and we rented a horse-drawn gypsy wagon which we slept in as we traveled the beautiful cobbled streets and lanes of the Irish countryside. We met interesting people everywhere we went, and I remember one instance where we'd traveled to a small village looking for a certain man I'd heard about who made chairs using straw and rope. We couldn't find him, and so I stopped in at one house to ask if they knew the gentleman-- and it turned out to be his house. This craftsman had about twelve kids, and he called them in from the fields to meet us. The kids were so shy they kind of hid behind the fences, watching us wide-eyed and curious.

Outside, the father showed us his way of turning straw into rope, and using it for the chairs and other furniture he made, that he sold to bring in some money for his family. Inside, the floor in their house was dirt, and cows and chickens seemed to have the run of the place. A heat-burning fireplace was used for both heating and cooking. They were delightful people, serving us Irish whiskey in Waterford glasses, and making us feel as welcome as they could. We took movies of our travels, and when I returned, I aired a number of travel segments on my television shows.

I think we were about three days into the deal with Aurora when I knew it was a mistake, although I wasn't able to actually do anything about it until a year later, around June 1970.

Throughout that year, I'd been thinking about ways I could get out of the contract. At the time, my attorneys, who I'd worked with over the years in Temple City, were telling me, "No, there's no way you can get out of the deal." But I knew that there were a number of things that Aurora hadn't done to keep their side of the bargain, so I decided to consult with another attorney.

A friend of mine had mentioned an attorney to me. His name was Emil Steck, an attorney from the old school, responsible, honest, and dependable. Mr. Steck at the time represented companies such as Lockheed and Carnation Milk, and my friend had only positive things to say about him. So I made an appointment to see him. After reviewing the documents and assessing the situation, Mr. Steck said to me, "I'll have you out of this deal in two weeks." Sure enough, he was as good as his word, and two weeks later the company was back in my hands!

Starting over a second time was fun, but it sure was harder. When you start out the first time, you're approaching it fresh, with an innocence. You do a lot of things automatically, without thinking them through. But when you build something up, as we had with Aleene's Tacky Glue and our other products, and watch it being torn down over a two-year period, you're starting over with someone else's wreckage. In addition to having changed the formula and the distinctive Aleene's Tacky Glue bottle, during the time Aurora owned the company many competitors had popped up in the market with their versions of "tacky glue." So I knew, going in, that there would be many more challenges the second time around. But I was so happy to have it back, that I remember saying to myself, "Well, the first time might have been youth and luck, but the second time is going to be experience and talent."

Gail stayed with Aurora right until the end, until the day we were officially released from contract to them. I'd already been off doing other things, since they weren't including me in their operations. But Gail tried to stay involved with Aurora, though his efforts weren't really appreciated by them either. Of course, that was a bone of contention between me and him, because I couldn't understand Gail's attitude about it all. He felt 100% responsible to live up to the contract, even though they had reneged on their end of the agreement.

Also, as I recall, Gail was against my taking back the company. He'd been negotiating with someone else to license Aleene's Tacky Glue. But I said "no," and I took the whole thing back against his wishes. In my mind, it was a fait accompli.

Aurora kept the product they were calling Mighty Tacky, then later sold it to one of the guys who worked for them. He, in turn sold, it to a company that still produces it.

But I felt certain that even though two years had gone by, I'd be able to come back into the market with a program of my own, and re-establish myself in a year or two, which is what I did. And I had fun doing it, never doubting for a moment that we'd be successful. For one thing, it seems to me that when things go bad, everybody sort of feels bad for you, like a sympathy vote. And I had a lot of friends in the industry who were upset with the Aurora deal, and who got behind me in my efforts to rebuild our business. Never doubt the importance of friends in this world, whether in business or in private life. And that wasn't the only time my friends got behind me and supported my effort. More recently, when I was under bankruptcy, which I'll tell you more about in a chapter coming up, I was able to contact my long-time friends and acquaintances in our field and obtain their help by asking them to pay for half of their orders up front, which is unheard of in the business. But I was able to do it because of their trust in me, and our long-standing reputation for living up to our word.

When I got Aleene's, Inc. back from Aurora, I didn't have much money at all to rebuild with. As a result, I had to cut a lot of things back, or cut them out completely. I couldn't do paint, for example, it was just too costly for me in my second "incarnation" as a business owner. In the past I'd been selling a variety of things, like velour crepe paper, tissue paper, and many other items. Now, starting out again, I knew I had to focus on my original tacky glue. I think I'd gotten about $60,000 from the Aurora deal, and I plunged all of it right into my new business. One of my first moves, of course, was to get back to my gold bottles, and the original formulation of our product.

By the way, I think that's one of the mistakes a lot of people make when they're starting out; doing too many things instead of taking one thing you do well and concentrating on it. There are so many things that come up that intrigue you, but you've really got to put the brakes on. Stop and think before you leap in and spread yourself too thin. It takes a lot of money to put a product on the market. You should do it in a small way at first. Maybe you're going to be copied, but you have to take the chance nonetheless. I had to do a lot of publicity, write a mountain of p.r. releases and go to shows by myself, as we didn't even have enough money for Gail to go with me. I taught at the shows, did "Make It and Take It" for the buyers, and I remember many times when I couldn't even leave the booth to eat lunch, because there was no one to spell me. I would do the promotion, set up the show, break it down, any and everything to make it work right, just like a one-woman band.

It was a lot more difficult to re-introduce a product that had once been so successful, than I'd imagined. And it took a lot of work. Fortunately, I'd never gone off television during all the trials and tribulations involving the sale to Aurora. Regardless of what was happening, I'd stayed very visible. During this period I was on the Dinah Shore Show, and many other shows. My high visibility on television was a strong advantage in my efforts to re-establish myself and my company in this new round.

One of the first things I did when I had the company back, was to contact a man named Tom Yaley, from Yaley Enterprises. (See photo of Candle Crafting Catalog & Books

I guested on a regular basis with celebrities like
Dinah Shore, seen above.

that we developed for Yaley in center insert.) I had been recommended to him as a top-notch marketing person. He came to talk to me about what we were doing, and he liked my approach to marketing so much that he decided to hire me to do marketing for his candle crafting products, their main business. Needing to bring in some income for our business, as a consultant to Yaley, I wrote candle crafting books for him, designed their whole packaging and marketing plans, and even did sales.

Our arrangement was a good one. We got a percentage of all we sold. And Tom was a very, very nice person to work with. His father owned a company called Paragon Wax Refining Co., a very old candle products company. His father also had a trucking concern and some other businesses. And when he died, Tom took over Paragon Wax. Tom didn't really know anything about the craft industry, so I was able to inform him about the in's and outs of the business, and to connect him to a lot of people in the field.

In January of 1971, I took Tom Yaley to the HIA Show to display his candle crafting products. I'd devoted about three months to getting his presentation ready for that show, and I know Tom was very pleased by what I'd done, and by the good response we got for it. At the same time, I showed something I called "Paint a Purdy Picture." (See photo of Recipe for Painting Paint a Purdy Picture, in center insert.) Recently, I've been developing that idea into "Recipe For Painting," which we're now licensing to Oxmoor House, our publishers. In addition to Yaley Enterprises, I remember I also took on a company called Plantabs, which packaged silica gel for drying flowers. I wrote a book for them, and did lots of odds and ends consulting work. I managed all this in addition to running and rebuilding my own company.

Over the years, I've always had people writing to me and sending me ideas, comments, and crafts suggestions. One day, a lady from Salt Lake City sent me a liver lid, and wrote, "put it in your oven and see what happens." So I did, and it shrank to a miniature. The liver lid was a round plastic lid that came on packages of liver. It had a little red design in the center of it. When it shrank, it shrank into an oval. It didn't shrink all that well, as I remember. In her letter, the lady from Salt Lake said it was very popular with her friends at craft night at their church, and that she just wanted to share the idea with me.

I said to Gail that I thought we should look into this plastic. I thought it was kind of interesting, and also thought that the plastic must be available somewhere. This kind of research was something Gail was good at and liked doing. He looked into where we could get that kind of plastic. He also researched how we could find a plastic that would shrink fairly evenly. There's still a 5% distortion in it now, after all the years of working to perfect it.

I remember that I drew a little Santa Claus, and some snowmen, and sent them off to our distributors and reps. I told them, "Put this stuff in your oven, bake it, and let me know what you think." Every one of them came back and said it wasn't any good. It made me angry, because I thought it was good. I decided to go around the country with it, from TV station to TV station. At that time, I didn't know how it was going to go, I hadn't used it on the air or demonstrated it at all myself. My husband took an oven and put a light in it so we could watch it shrinking. The first place I stopped was Phoenix. People went crazy, absolutely crazy about it. I did it on a morning show and a noon or afternoon show. By the time I left there to go to the next stop, I knew we had a winner. We didn't have it packaged or anything. We didn't even have an instruction book, just the idea and the demonstration of it. After the Phoenix show, I just phoned back and said, "We've got it! The people like it!" We didn't have it packaged until I got to, Atlanta, Georgia, for the show.

My son Fred, who is our plant manager, came along with me on that Shrink-Art trip. We bought a brand new Ford van, right at the height of the gas crisis, as I recall, that had a 50-gallon tank on it. Everything was loaded into cartons that I'd had specially put up, and all the samples were mounted on panels for easy display. Fred recalls that we had 33 cartons with us, which he unloaded at each stop and set-up for me. That first Shrink-Art show in Phoenix was held at the Holiday Inn. I'd gone on local television the day before, and to my happy surprise, we had a mob scene at the Holiday Inn the next day. People loved the product. During this trip, which, like the Craft Caravan, was also about six

"Shrink-It," formally known as "Shrink-Art," was number 1 on the Craft Hit Parade for 4-5 years, and is still the number 1 kids craft project.

months, we hit a number of important trade shows, from Phoenix to Atlanta to Philadelphia. Fred stayed on the road with the van, while I flew home every so often. Then, I'd fly back to meet up with him in the next city on our route, he'd pick me up at the airport, and off we went. It was grueling in some respects, but with the acceptance of our newest product, Shrink Art, it was worth it.

By the time we reached Atlanta, Gail had located the best producers of the plastic. Everyone back at our plant was working day and night, and even weekends, packaging Shrink Art to send out to our customers. As quickly as we could package it, out the door it went!

*

During the summer of 1971 we went on a covered wagon trek through Kansas. I took all the children. It was a great trip that gave us some ideas of the feelings that the pioneers had when they crossed the United States going west. One of the only concessions to modern times, was a restroom on one of the covered wagons. Everything else was as close to the old ways as possible. We all put on costumes at night when we came into camp and cooked out over open fires. There was entertainment of the kind they probably had in the old days, designed to give you the feelings and the experiences of what it might have been like to be one of the earliest pioneers.

We rode the Old Chisholm Trail, and I bet we experienced a lot of what the pioneers might have gone through. We had every kind of weather, from freezing cold to really hot; wind, rain, you name it. The trip lasted about six days. Near the last day, we reached a place called Castle Rock, the highest point in Kansas. It's off the highway maybe two or three miles. For some reason, it's a popular spot in Kansas, and there were a bunch of cars up there on top of this little mountain. Can you imagine their surprise when they saw an old time covered wagon train coming toward them? We got to the top, we invited the people in the cars to come join us for dinner.

To me, all these things made it a very special trip for me and my family. Anytime I could find something unusual, which sometimes took some doing, I would go for it. Especially if it was something I could involve the kids in. This, to me, was what education was really supposed to be about.

This was our second covered wagon trip that we took. The first was a historical trek through Kansas. The second, shown above, was through the Grand Tetons. Both were family affairs, as I invited my children and their families to participate.

This is a sampling of several of the first kits that Artis/Aleene's produced. Included above are: Shrink-Art, Hand-Tiques and Hi*Dye Batik and Dyeing.

Books, Kits and Products.

There have been so many different projects that we at Aleene's have initiated through the years, that I have decided to do this section as a pictorial review of some of the highlights. And were starting with a grouping of Aleene's Catalogs. We started printing catalogs in the early days of the Formosan Wood Fibre craze. This was before the craft industry took off, but during the time when Aleene's was featured in Life Magazine as, "one of the fastest growing companies in the United States." As new flower-making materials became popular, sales of Wood Fibre decreased and Aleene's began going into the many different craft categories that you will see on the next pages.

There were many eras of book publication, starting with 50¢ and 60¢ books and progressing into today's beautiful four-color creations.

You will see pictures of the first two hard-bound books published, and also today's books, such as *Aleene's Big Book of Crafts*, published by Oxmoor House.

You will get a peek at some of the idea sheets we offered through the many years, at no charge. Of course this program has grown into the Aleene's Craft Club, a monthly subscription mailing of 50 or more idea sheets including, not only Aleene's projects, but those of our guests on our television show.

You will see books and kits for projects such as: Shrink-Art (Shrink-It), Tole Painting, Candle Crafting, Batik and Dyeing, Styrofoam®, Beading, and Preserving Flowers. This is not even a fraction of the programs that we have been involved in. It's just a few that I could find some pictures to illustrate.

Every year, for 40+ years, we have created at least 1 catalog.
Perhaps you will recognize one you've used from the assortment
shown.

Shown are a few of the 100+ books that we had with us on the Craft Caravan. The sale of these books financed our trip.

We decided to publish 99¢ books. They were low cost and full-color
enhancing the sale of certain Aleene's products.

These are the original "Crafts for Kids" books developed to teach kids of all ages how to craft.

Shown here are the original series of books.

Shown are the newest books edited by Tiffany. These are currently available through our distributor Leisure Arts.

Treasures From Trash was my first hardbound book published by Hearthside Press. *Super Scrap Craft* was a combined effort of Aleene, Tiffany and Heidi, published by New America Publishing Co.

Aleene, Tiffany and Heidi collaborated with Oxmoor House on
Aleene's famous *Big Book of Crafts* and the three books shown.
Several new ones are on the way.

Everyone always asks me "What is your favorite craft, Aleene?"
My first choice is Christmas, followed by Bread Dough and
Burnt Brown Bag.

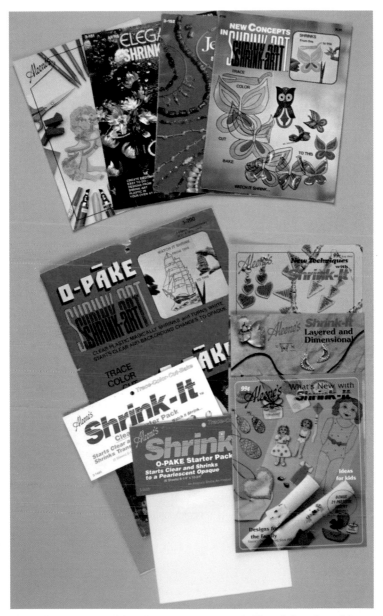

Shrink-Art started by shrinking a "liver lid" and developed into the most popular "kids craft" of the century. We now call it Aleene's Shrink-It and it includes both the clear plastic and the opake plastic.

When I sold Aleene's to Aurora, I decided to learn to paint. The result was my collaboration with a gentleman named Don Purdy. Our first book called "Paint a Purdy Picture," renamed "Recipe for Painting."

I originally started with a free design pamphlet called "The Petal Pusher." Through the years this developed into free idea-sheets that were sent to viewers who sent in a self-addressed stamped envelope. Now the sheets are part of the new Aleene's Craft Club.

Leisure Arts, is a division of Oxmoor House. They have taken designs from *Aleene's Big Book of Crafts*, and re-released them into paperback form.

Flower Dri, a product packaged by Plantabbs Corp., was one of my first clients. I wrote the book *Preserve Your Posies*, designed packaging, promoted and sold the product.

Hi*Dye was a product I promoted for LeJuene Inc. later I pur-
chased the company and packaged the dye and Batik Wax. I wrote
the books *"Batik and Dyeing"* and *"Sneak Batik."*

I became interested in tole and decorative painting. My husband and I, visiting Sturbridge Village Library, created hand soldered reproductions of early American tinware. I collaborated with a tole painter on the book *"Tole Painting Made Easy."*

Another client of mine was Tom Yaley of Yaley Ent. Candle Crafting. For this company I designed the packaging, the marketing plan and did sales. Our company created the plastic and metal molds for pouring candles. I also designed and authored four candle crafting books.

Having been the first person in the floral and craft industry, to discover STYROFOAM®, (manufactured by DOW Chemical Co.) I soon became a spokesperson and consultant for Dow and produced the first two books on STYROFOAM®.

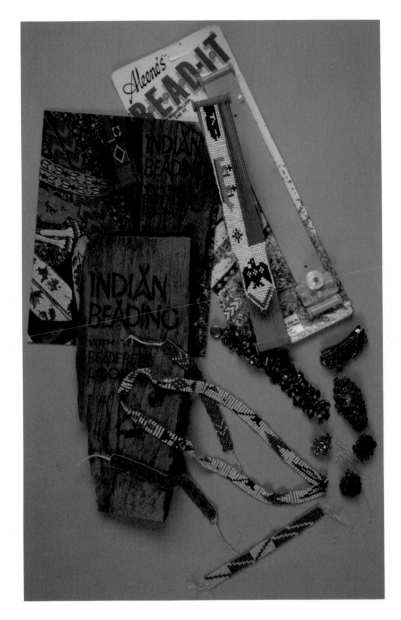

Many years ago we bought the patent for the Indian beading loom. Ultimately the name was changed to "Beaderette," and then to its current name, "Bead-It." As we found out, we could do very elegant jewelry without the limitations of conventional looms.

Creative Living Magazines, from past to present.

Tony was thirteen when we moved to the country, to the beautiful Santa Ynez Valley in southern California. This was a dream come true!

CHAPTER SEVEN

Moving to the Country

Each of us has a dream, probably more than one, usually kept simmering somewhere on the back burner. We hope it's going to come true some day, and in many cases, it does. For a long time, my dream had to do with horses, with being in the country, and living close to nature. I'd been dreaming about having horses ever since my childhood days when I used to "live" at the stables, horseback riding whenever I could. To have my own horses, on my own land, was a dream I'd kept on the back burner all those years since childhood, and, in early '70s, after I'd gotten the company back from Aurora and our business was starting to rebuild, I got my chance.

I'm not sure when we first started "looking," but Gail and I had in mind finding a place where we could keep horses, and one that would also have any airfield close by for him. I think I'd been fantasizing about a dude ranch type of place, where we could fly up for the weeks, ride, and then fly back to Temple City to our business. We'd even flown in Gail's Bonanza out to see such a ranch near Phoenix, Arizona, and while it was nice, it didn't strike me as the place for me. So I kept looking.

One of our trips brought us up to the beautiful town of Santa Ynez, in the horse country of northern Santa Barbara County. Oddly enough, it was just up the road from Refugio Beach, north of Santa Barbara, the place where Gail and I had once stopped when we were first spending time together. That was the time he convinced me that we were destined for each other, and that I should divorce Woody and marry him. Now it was some four or so years later, and we were back up in that neck of the woods again, this time looking at properties.

Both Gail and I liked the area. The lovely village of Solvang, settled by people from Denmark who've kept up Danish customs and traditions, is surrounded by rolling green hills so perfect for horses. I'd left my card with a real estate lady, and one day I got a call from her, telling me to come back up. She had something special to show me. She was an unusual woman, very active in a lot of different things. I knew she had the knack for putting people together with places they'd like. That, to me, is what being a real estate person is all about. She said she had a "little ranch" to show me, not a dude ranch as we'd talked about. I told her we were still looking at other parts of California, and that we hadn't settled on Santa Barbara County. But she encouraged me by saying, "Why don't you come up anyway, we'll go out for wine and cheese, and have a picnic."

We drove up for the weekend right after Christmas, 1973, and, of course, it was gorgeous up here. The rains had come, and the grass was up to the cows' bellies. The real estate gal showed us a couple of places, including one that

A picture of the U-shaped house in Fredensborg Canyon.

All that you could see from our little ranch were
horses and cows grazing.

had a tennis court and swimming pool, but they didn't move
me at all. Then, a little later that afternoon, she took us to
see a place in Fredensborg Canyon, which I fell in love with.

The house on Fredensborg Canyon Road was U-
shaped, with solid glass all around. Its windows looked out
onto the green hills of Santa Ynez. I could see hillsides with
horses and cows grazing, trees, a couple of red-tailed hawks,
and a countryside which was as pleasing to the soul as it was
to the eye. In the family room was a walk-in-sized fireplace.
In the front room, I had my desk to the window, where I
would later sit and watch a line of baby quail filing by in
front of the house. (That fireplace turned out to be the only
source of heat in the house, so later on, when we lived there,
I had to use electric heaters.) There were three bedrooms and
also a guest apartment. All told, the property came with 20
acres, ten on one piece, ten on another. To me, it was like
heaven. There's no other way to put it, it just felt like heav-
en.

The house had been built by a Santa Barbara couple,
a school teacher and her husband who worked for the coun-

ty water department. They were delightful people who'd put a lot of love into building that house. Everything about it was so special, so beautiful. I loved their ideas, their style and the way they'd put so much thought into everything they did to it. Little things, I guess, like painting each individual tongue-and-groove board before putting them into place, things like that. They'd called it "Bird Track Hill," and I liked the name so much I kept it. I still have the wooden sign that announced "Bird Track Hill" to visitors coming up the drive.

As I recall, on our way driving south to Temple City that evening, I decided I was going to buy the place. The price was around $130,000, It was a good price at the time, although it was steeper than what I'd had in mind to pay. At the time, I'd sold my interest in the Snowfoam plant, so I knew I had some money to work with. Gail had virtually no money to speak of, so buying "Bird Track Hill" was really my decision to make. Finally, as we were approaching Los Angeles, I told him I was definitely going to buy it. I'd made up my mind. I think I also said I was going to drive back up the next day and clinch the deal.

At first, Gail objected. But as I discussed it with him into the night, he started to think positively about it. After all, there was an airfield nearby, and he liked the idea of flying to work and back every day. It's a good thing too, because he ended up doing just that for about two years!

The next morning, back in Temple City, I told my dad that I'd seen a place I was going to buy. He told me I was crazy. My business was only just back on the road to recovery after the Aurora Debacle, and dad wasn't the only one who cautioned me against it. Quite a few people close to me expressed their concerns, but I was going to buy that house regardless! I guess I'm that way--once my mind is made up, I usually go for it, whatever it happens to be.

A couple of days later, just before New Year's Eve, I signed the papers and Bird Track Hill was mine. I didn't move up until the following Mother's Day because I was out on the caravan for a couple of months. But I was thinking about the place the whole time I was out on the road, so looking forward to moving in.

I still owned our building in Temple City that housed

the business, then called Artis/Aleene. Aurora had kept the name for a time, and I had to fight to legally get it back. In the short run, I used the name Artis/Aleene. Don't ask me where Artis came from, though, I just pulled it out of the air. During the Aurora period, they'd rented the building from us, but now that I'd gotten out of the contract, the building belonged to me. It was mine to do with as I pleased. And in this case, that meant selling it. We had about forty employees working for us down in Temple City. At that time our business involved a lot of packaging; things like Shrink Art, which had taken off in a big way; and our other products including candle molds and, of course, my tacky glue, the original formula, in its original gold bottle. I knew that eventually I wanted to move the business up to Santa Ynez, but first I moved myself into the house at Bird Track Hill on Mother's Day, 1974. But first I settled in the house and in the surrounding community. Gail continued to fly back and forth every day, managing the company down in Temple City, while I did sales and other promotional work by phone

"A pot of gold at the end of the rainbow," was truly ours at Fredensborg canyon.

from Santa Ynez. When the need arose, I would fly down with Gail, or drive down for special meetings at the plant.

Fredensborg was a wonderful breath of fresh air for me, and the surrounding community couldn't have been better. Within a week of moving in, I advertised in the local newspaper offering a series of free classes in crafts, and over 200 people showed up! I met a lot of delightful people that way, many of them neighbors, from artists to business people, and very quickly I made some really good friends.

As I said, I knew I wanted to move my business up to the Santa Ynez area, but at the same time, there just wasn't any place to have a plant. This was rural, horse and cow country, and while there was lots and lots of open space, there weren't any buildings that could house a business like mine. So I started looking for property to build on. I found a piece of land that I thought would be perfect, on a street called Industrial Way, in the town of Buellton, just over from Santa Ynez. It was right near the freeway, which was important to us with all the trucks coming in and out, and something about it felt right to me instantly. The only problem was that the owner, Andy Petersen, had no desire to sell any of his land. He was warm to the idea of putting up a building himself, and leasing it to us, but I kept saying no. I wanted to buy the property. It's something I like to do, if and when I can. As a friend of mine once said, "buy land, they've quit making it."

I persisted with Andy Petersen, stopping in on him maybe every couple of weeks. I've got to say that trying to get someone to sell me a property is something I consider fun. One day, after I'd been bugging him for about a year-and-a-half, I said, "Are you going to sell this land to me?" I think he wasn't feeling all that well on that day, when he replied, "Okay, I'll do it." I knew his word was as good as could be. We shook hands on it and the deal was clinched. And, of course, Gail had a fit.

Everybody was totally surprised that Andy had agreed to sell me the five acre parcel, after all, he'd been so adamant about not selling it to me for so long. Even his son, a very nice gentleman who has since taken over the management of his father's properties, couldn't believe it. But Andy was as good as his word, and the land was mine.

Immediately, we started to make plans for our building. Gail was very good when it came to observing things like buildings, construction in general, any big projects involving design work. We used to drive down to Los Angeles quite often. Gail would point out every new building along the way. Nothing escaped him. It's a gift I wish I had, because I know I miss a lot. He never missed anything. Gail was the kind of guy who was always looking, always seeing, always learning how things worked. Along with the local contractor, Gail had designed our building. I oversaw most of the construction because he was still flying down to our plant in Temple City every day. Then, in short order, I arranged to sell our building down south to finance the construction in Buellton. My dad had owned one of our Temple City buildings, which he'd sold to a refrigeration company, and I owned the other one. As I began planning to move Artis/Aleene's up to Buellton, I knew we were going to have to trim down our personnel. We'd have to hire people from our new location, since it was too far for anyone to commute, anyone without an airplane, that is.

This was the original building in Buellton, California, for Aleene's, Division of Artis Inc. Over the years, it has grown to over six times it's original size.

Moving a company is no small feat, let me tell you. My son Fred remembers that it was about two years, from when I bought the land to when we actually had a finished building and were able to move into it in 1976. In that time, there were designs to be completed, permits to be obtained, problems to overcome, and a million-and-a-half other details to work out.

*

It was 1976 when the company finally got moved up here to Buellton. It was also that year that the National Craft Association was launched as an alternative to the Hobby Industry Association. It was started by a gentleman down in Texas who originally had the idea. He was furious with the Hobby Industry Association, and he wasn't the only one. He got a group of us together who were crafts people and who thought that our industry should have its own trade association, with the word "crafts" in its name, an idea I had been pushing for quite some time you'll recall. This group included the publisher of the *Profitable Crafts Merchandising* magazine, among others. These were big people in the industry getting together to say the hobby industry was never going to recognize us. They were never going to work with us as we wanted them to, so, we might as well have our own organization.

For one thing, the HIA was always charging us a lot of money for booths at their trade shows. Most of the members of this group felt that we should have our own association instead of paying them all that money. And so we started having meetings. At the first meeting, Gail was voted president of the group. I think, in some ways, our forming this group was the beginning of the hobby association recognizing the craft people. They knew that they had better start spending some of the dues money toward things that would benefit the crafts industry, not just the hobby model industry. At this point, the craft industry probably represented 50% of the dues structure of the HIA, yet they still didn't want to wake up to the fact. If I'm not mistaken, the HIA had virtually no craftspeople on its board of directors.

Our new organization took off for a time. We had

two national trade shows, and they were very good. Just about that time, the Hobby Industry Association started to get worried about us, I guess. They began to convince people that we didn't need two different associations. Suddenly, the HIA started listening to what we had been saying for so long; that crafts were getting the short end of the stick, even though the crafts field was growing by leaps and bounds, while the model industry was dying a not-so-slow death. So, I guess everybody decided, including ourselves, that if the HIA was going to finally listen to us, there was probably no reason to continue trying to get our National Crafts Association going.

However, because Gail was president of this upstart association, and because I was an outspoken advocate for more promotion of crafts in the HIA, they weren't easy for me to do business with. The following year, as I remember, they assigned me a booth at the HIA show that was on top of the freight elevator. This meant I couldn't set up my booth until after all the freight was up. The year after, they gave me a booth with a great big post in the center of it. It was always something that they did that rankled me, and too often I sensed it wasn't a mere coincidence.

Another problem between me and the HIA occurred as a result of my selling to Aurora. When we finally parted company, as I said, Aurora kept the name Aleene's, and it took me almost two years to get it back. But according to the HIA bylaws, a company would get points for the amount of time they'd exhibited with the association and for the amount of space that you took each time. But they refused to give me credit for that. They threw out all the points I'd accumulated before the Aurora sale, even though my company never stopped being in business or participating in their activities. I almost felt like I had to get an attorney again to try to regain my standing with them. And the worst part about it is, they won't tell you how many points you have. This can be important to a company like mine, because placement of your booth is linked to the number of points your company has racked up. The person with the most points gets first choice. I really should be the second or third in the craft group after all our years participating with them, but by their reckoning I'm down around 19th or 20th! It's another one of those ongoing battles, I guess, with me in the forefront of trying to get recognition for the crafts industry, as I've always done over the years. Ironically, as I've mentioned before, the Hobby Industry Association today is about 90% crafts, and about 10% hobby models, if that!

*

I was anxious to move my whole family up to Buellton, but it didn't quite work out that way; at least, not at first. Heidi had married Jimmy, her first husband, and had started a family of her own. She'd taken over my retail store down south, moving it to another location after we sold the building in Temple City. She was also doing a mail order business with my parents. Tiffany, who was around nineteen at the time, was planning to come up with us. She liked horses, and knew we would have stables at Bird Track Hill. But as the time approached, love played a hand, and she married Randy Windsor. They decided to stay in the Los Angeles

This was Heidi's first marriage to Jimmy Hall. Candy was the Maid of Honor, Tiffany, the Junior Brides Maid and Tony, the Ring Bearer.

area. My older son, Fred, who'd just returned from two years in the Coast Guard, was instrumental in the move. He came up with me, but took an apartment in town. Candy, as I've mentioned, was on the East Coast. So that left Tony, who was thirteen, living with Gail and me in the house. For a time Fred lived in the little apartment on the property. Then Heidi came there for a while. Looking back on it, it seemed to me like everyone stayed in that apartment at one time or another.

It was around that time that Fred, who used the name Rick, took a vacation to Scotland with a friend of his, who was an antique buyer. While they were over there, Fred met a woman named Connie, who was in the antique exporting business with her brother. I remember Fred calling

Tiffany and her husband Randy.

me from Scotland to let us know he was going to stay there for a while. Then, a few weeks later, he called to say he and Connie were getting married. It was his first marriage, her second. Fred was twenty-eight or so at the time, and I decided we should all go over there to help celebrate the wedding.

Going to Fred and Connie's wedding in Scotland also gave me an opportunity to visit parts of Europe that were new to me, like Switzerland. I was delighted by the Swiss people and the country as a whole. We'd been importing a material called Swistraw from a company over there, and I'd always wanted to see their factory. Swistraw was a synthetic type of raffia which was used in flower-making, weaving, crocheting and all kinds of things. The company was at least 100 years old, and situated in a beautiful old building from the 1800s. They made a lot of products for hats and things other than crafts.

We went all over Switzerland on that trip, and of all the places in the world that I've visited, Switzerland is the best. It's fantastic, really; a dream world with beautiful mountains and exquisite little villages tucked away in them. In every village, I saw beautiful flowers. And I was amazed at how clean it was throughout Switzerland as a whole. We drove quite a ways, as I remember, and then went through Italy and France. We ended up on the French border, and then over the French Alps to Paris. That's when I realized that some of the myths about the unfriendly French, have a basis in reality. They were hardly friendly to us, in fact, just the opposite. I had to collect a bill in Paris. But I was amazed at how seemingly rude Parisians were to foreigners like us. In Montmarte, we stayed in a really cute little hotel. Then we crossed the channel into England. Tony and his girlfriend were with us, and for fun, when we went to Scotland a few days before Fred and Connie's wedding. We went up to Loch Ness to look for the famous monster.

After the wedding, Fred and Connie stayed in Scotland, where they were planning to live permanently. The wedding was in September, and a few months later, in January, Fred called me at an HIA show saying he and Connie wanted to come home to the U.S., and did I have a job for him? I said, sure, and helped them come back over here and get settled near our home on Bird Track Hill.

After we'd gotten settled in Buellton, I pretty much had to hire all new people. Aside from my family, the only one of our crew who moved up to Buellton with us was my bookkeeper, Joe Medina. He was always quick, and one of the best people I've ever had work with me. At the time, we were still rebuilding after the Aurora debacle, and since it wasn't a really big business, hiring new people to replace the ones we'd left down south wasn't too difficult.

We'd set up our multilith press in the new building, and continued publishing our books. I was big into "junk" crafts then; promoting the notion that there were plenty of "found" materials around the average person's home that could be turned into beautiful crafts with not too much effort. Looking through one of my many boxes of clippings

Fred and his wife Connie. married in Scotland. A chance for our family to tour Europe.

and saved memorabilia of my life in the crafts industry, I'm taken with an issue of *Craft Ideas* that we published in 1974.

Those of you reading this who knew of our work back then, will remember that I introduced "Burnt Brown Bags," which became a very popular item. This craft involved using discarded brown paper bags to create beautiful artwork that had the look of antiqued bronze or metal. My designer, a great lady named Katie Ogle, had come up with the idea. While testing the glues for flammability, she came up with the way to make it look like metal. In a lot of ways, Katie was also a mentor to my daughter Heidi; teaching Heidi the basics of designing and pointing her in the right direction. (Sadly, Katie died in a plane crash a few years later, while flying with Gail up to San Francisco for a business meeting. Gail survived that one.)

In the introduction to that issue of *Craft Ideas*, (which sold for $1.50!), I wrote, "Some of the designs feature craft media such as Swistraw, felt, paint, glue, transfer medium, STYROFOAM® (since the company insisted that the word appear in all capital letters), and Shrink-art, items you would purchase at your local Craft Store. However, most of the items used are JUNK, things that you would ordinarily discard. Simply elegant things can be made from brown grocery bags, pine cones, paper, leaves, cleansing tissues and bottle caps. By learning how to work with the materials, you can achieve a professional effect. In this day and age where everything is so expensive, you will save money by creating your own designs and gifts and you will be able to create things that are professional enough to sell through your church, school, or other organization, or through your own effort, to make money." I wrote that about twenty-two years ago, and all of it is still true today.

That issue also had burnt brown bag designs, such as an old sailing ship pattern and an eagle pattern. The materials needed were Aleene's Tacky White Glue, a gold acrylic matte spray paint, .22-gauge bare wire, gold tissue paper and clear glue. In that issue I also showed projects from bottle caps, cans and containers; things you could do with plastic spoons, melting them over candles and using the new shapes for plastic flowers; inexpensive wire garden baskets wrapped with Swistraw; simple Bargello picture frames or

Beachcraft Bonanza 5000 Bravo after being retrieved from the bottom of the San Fransico Bay. Accident due to air traffic controller's lack of spacing behind a 747 in the fog.

bags which were made from stitchery on canvas using Swistraw; shag flowers, and other items also made using Swistraw; as well as instructions on how to make an inexpensive loom using an old picture frame and dowels for stretcher bars. Among other things, we were packaging Shrink-art, which we now call Shrink It. It was the kind of thing anyone could do with a little training. And I must say, we've always been able to hire excellent people from the Buellton area, so that's never been a problem.

What did turn out to be a problem, however, was our venture into Tin-Ware. You'll recall that I'd been involved with Yaley Enterprises in the candle business. Through them we'd made contact with a small company, O'Laughlin Manufacturing, down in Temecula, about an hour or so southeast of Los Angeles. Mr. O'Laughlin was making candle molds, and was looking to retire. Gail got interested in the field, and as I recall, my son Fred went down to Temecula for about three weeks, to learn how to set up punch presses, brakes and shears, and how to make candle molds. We bought out O'Laughlin, and then moved the equipment up to the new plant in Buellton, and set it up there. We had a good feeling about Tin-Ware and tole painting on metal, so Gail and I flew back to Sturbridge, Massachusetts, where they had an antique museum and library from the late 1700s showing a variety of kitchen items made from tin. We took photographs and Gail made sketches of a number of these items. And when we got back to California, we started to produce them on the machinery we bought from O'Laughlin.

We made a really great line of Tin-Ware reproductions, including milk carton containers, large and small grain scoops, napkin rings, cups, caddies, and breadbox bins of several sizes. When we were up and running with the Tin-Ware, I published a book called *Tole Painting* (Painting on Tin) *Made Easy* showing the Artis Tin-Ware reproductions and tole painting designs that anyone could do on tin. Tole Painting, sometimes called Pennsylvania Dutch Tole, or Primitive Folk Art, used the "comma" as it's basic stroke, and for a time was a very popular craft. I'd first gotten interested in it during the period when Aurora owned us. I met a talented young designer, Beverly Cook, and took one of her first classes in tole painting. Beverly and I then went on to develop a printed method where people, whether talented or not, could learn to paint the two hundred year old Pennsylvania Dutch Tole designs on our tin products, or even on wood if they so chose. It was immensely popular, and I felt we'd picked another winner.

But two things happened to derail our tin operation. First, Gail insisted on trying to market and distribute it through existing distribution systems. But by the time it finally got to the consumer, the cost was too high. I wanted to go direct to the consumer because I'd presented Tin-Ware at some craft shows and everyone found that everyone liked it. I knew if the price was right, that is, low, I'd be able to sell it. But I couldn't sell it if I had to sell to a distributor who in turn sold it to a dealer, who in turn sold it to the final customer. Too much mark-up spoiled that broth. But when Gail had his mind made up about something, like going through the existing distribution channels, forget it!

The other negative thing that happened to Tin-Ware was that the government, in the form of the Occupation

One of our staff, hand-soldering reproductions of
Early American Tinware.

Safety & Health Administration (OSHA), decided that some
of our machines posed a possible threat to the workers. I had
to re-do the knobs on one of the machines, because, according to the OSHA inspector, it represented a hazard to the
employees. We went ahead and did it. This little correction
cost us over $5,000, and we weren't done yet. About six
months later, the OSHA inspector came back to see us and
told me the knobs still weren't out far enough! I couldn't
believe it when he said they would have to be moved another couple of inches. I told him I wouldn't do it. We weren't
making enough profit from Tin-Ware to justify the ongoing
expense of re-building the machinery to their specifications.
I told the inspector that if he was insistent, I would simply
shut down that part of my plant. He said, "Okay, if that's
what you're going to do, go ahead and do it." So I did. That
very afternoon, I called the Tin-Ware workers together and
said, "I just can't continue with these restrictions they're
putting on us, so I guess we're going to have to stop producing Tin-Ware." The workers weren't too happy about it,
of course, and that afternoon I gave them their final checks.

I wasn't too happy about it myself, because I liked the product, in spite of the difficulties. But I'm not one to hang on to things. So when it was over, it was over and we were moving on to the next project.

One of our staff, punching out Tjanting Pens for our Batiking and Dyeing lines.

Artis, Inc., manufactured a line of "primed Tin-ware Ready to Decorate."

Back at the ranch at "Tialto Family Farms," when we began shooting the television show at the new setting.

CHAPTER EIGHT

Troubles in Paradise

It isn't easy to write about the difficulties in your life, but I feel I must tell you about them, as well as about the good times. One of the bad times came in early October of 1978, when Gail announced he was leaving me; that he wanted to "experience life" apart from me, as he put it.

We'd had our problems, like all couples with very few exceptions, I'm sure. And like all couples, it was hard for us to talk about the problems, to work them through. One of our biggest problems, as I've mentioned, is that Gail had to be the absolute ruler of his household, whereas I thought it should be a joint reign.

Another ongoing problem had to do with Gail's feelings about the way I was raising Tony, who was thirteen when we first moved up to Buellton. Unlike the older kids who were already out the door and on their own Tony lived with us. Gail thought I was spoiling Tony, and had felt this way since our earliest days together. Gail believed that adults were always right and that there was no room for discussion about anything from the kids' point of view. And he wouldn't just say something, with him you either did it or you got hit. Which I felt this wasn't fair to a child and I told him so. I had hoped to raise my kids the way my dad had raised me, but that didn't happen. At times, I protected the kids from him, another thing Gail didn't like.

It's true that I favored Tony, and I'm sure it was because I felt that of my five kids, he was the most like me. I thoroughly enjoyed watching Tony growing up and always felt happy to support him in whatever he was doing. Tony was always busy, ambitious in a good way, active, and just gung-ho about everything. Like myself, Tony liked horses a whole lot, and was riding from childhood. Early on in his high school years, Tony got a job working at the cattleyard auctions every Thursday. He'd arranged to get out of school at noon on that day and would head down there, often working until close to midnight. He was really interested in livestock auctions, and worked at the yard for a long time. Even when he came to work for Artis/Aleene, Inc., he still kept that Thursday job at the yard. His interest was so strong, that later he went back east to an auctioneering school to take courses on the subject.

Naturally, I wanted to help Tony in whatever he was doing. He was always helpful to me. Perhaps I did too much for him, I don't know. At least that's what Gail believed, and he certainly never hesitated to make his feelings known, both to Tony and to me. I remember one time, in particular, when Tony had some excess items from one of the auctions and I let him store them at our warehouse. Gail hit the roof, going on and on about how I was spoiling Tony. Naturally enough, troubles at home also spilled over into troubles in our business life together.

Tony was going to be a auctioneer, but ended up as president of Aleene's, Div. of Artis.

On that day in October, 1978, when Gail told me he was leaving, we'd been married not quite thirteen years. The last six were characterized by many battles and discontent between us. And Gail's feelings about my spoiling Tony were the most pronounced. On the day he announced to me that he had "had enough" of our life together, and that he wanted to separate, I was unhappy about it. But I, too, had sensed it coming. After the first few weeks that he moved out, we began to "see" each other about once a week, but it was awkward and strange. I was suddenly confronted by the reality that not only was he breaking up our marriage, but also our business, a business that we'd been building together, through the good times and the bad, for over a dozen years.

Before I started writing this chapter, I looked back through some old diaries of mine from that period. I want to bring in some of those pages right here, because I know that many of my feelings aren't unique, that many women have gone through similar things:

November 13, 1978: It has been a month since Gail moved out. Tonight I decided to put onto paper my feelings which are still very mixed.

In the first week or two, I felt the separation was good. It gave me time to breathe, to think. I had hoped it would give Gail time to also decide the good and the bad of our life together, and hopefully to work out some things which he felt he had to do. When he moved down to Van Nuys, I still felt that three more months were needed to work out our problems.

Until tonight, I opened the door many times to talk and to work on solving our problems. As of tonight, though, he will have to knock. Knowing Gail, he is very stubborn. Once he made the decision to leave, he couldn't back. His demands to rule Tony and myself ran against my conscience, and I couldn't back down either.

The advantages to separation: I have found I still have ability to do, think, to make decisions at work. To run Artis, Inc., successfully. To understand business. I am once more alive. I had almost forgotten what it was like to be in control of my life. And while Gail didn't dominate me, we seemed to both cancel each other out. In this separation, I find I am back amongst the living-- and liking people better. When we got married 13 years ago, it seems like I shut out a lot of the world and just devoted my life to Gail.

The disadvantages of separation: Being 55 years old and alone for the first time in about thirty-five years, is frightening. I love Gail in my own way, and I'm sure I will not find anyone as honest as he is. My pleasures will have to come from experiences I find by myself, and with my family.

I want adventure, joy, peace, and discovery. I want work to be but a part of my life. I still want to build and dec-

orate a house that is me. I don't see this as a threat to Gail, but he does.

I would still like to fulfill a dream of ten years, on a ranch/farm. To learn all about stock, growing and doing ranch chores. I don't mind at all giving up Bird Track Hill, which I had already decided to sell before we were separated because of the 90-unit development they're putting in next door. In some ways, it never fulfilled its purpose. It could have been ideal. I'm sorry I wasn't strong enough to make it so. It was a beautiful house, with an incredible view, and it could have been further developed. I plan on my own to make this dream come true, but maybe on a smaller scale.

I am once again back out with people. I don't know yet why I became so antagonistic to them, since I've loved entertaining, and I always enjoy learning about people. I hope that as a single girl I am able to further this. It would have been easier as a couple.

I will not go back in marriage to Gail unless by some miracle he changed his philosophy, and this is unrealistic and unlikely. I have good feelings for him, enjoy sleeping with him, but I can't go back to being owned by him. Now, I am at peace with myself, I like the feeling of independence again, and while it is lonesome, I guess it is better than the other way. I am Aleene again. Somewhere along the line I had lost my identity.

Fifth Month: Gail comes to visit on weekends to discuss business and our divorce. I want to keep the doors open, but I wonder if you can ever get it back with someone? Can you ever forget all the building up of the bad things? Can you ever stop bringing up things that happened in the past?

I wrote another letter to him, but I didn't send it. I write usually after we're together for a night or weekend. Most of my letters show defeat and despair, so I don't send them. I have always been a very self-reliant person, so I am relying on that part of me. Today, a call came from a girlfriend whom I assisted, over thirty years ago, during her unhappy divorce. She said she had heard about mine, but was happy knowing it "wouldn't affect me all that much" since I was so strong. (What about those lonely nights I cried...?)

Went to a town meeting tonight. I never minded going alone before, but somehow, being separated now, makes me feel like I stand out as a leper. Wives look at you, a separated woman, as possible competition for their husbands. And men are just plain afraid to talk to you.

I'm writing this after having stayed up all night with you again. I find myself tied up in a knot all the time, always apprehensive. It's been five months since you decided to leave-- four months you've been living down in Van Nuys. While you seem much more at ease with me recently, every time I mention something we did wrong in the past, you still think I am singling you out. This is not true. I made as many mistakes, and I admit it.

You've told me of your experiences while we've been apart, and I wonder about how it will be if we ever get back together, knowing you could meet someone at any moment who would change things. And I could too. In a way, it's sort of like working for someone when you know you could be fired, or that the company go bankrupt at any moment. You can't quite give your best under those conditions.

*

If anyone told me today that their husband was leaving them, I would recommend they don't say anything nasty during the separation. Really, I'm serious. If you don't say anything nasty, you don't bring up things that can later come back to haunt you. Of course, I didn't like keeping my anger to myself, and I took my frustrations out by going down to the beach and sitting and writing in my diary.

During the nearly seven months that Gail and I were separated, I did a lot of exploring, in addition to a lot of soul searching. I sold Bird Track Hill, mainly because someone was going to build a development of 90 homes right next to it. Since I had twenty acres, I subdivided it into four parcels and made a good profit on it. Tony helped me quite a bit on that. And later, I helped him buy his own house in town. Tony was also becoming more and more active at our shop. With Gail out of it completely, I really needed the help. When Gail left for those seven months, he left me with a business that was in trouble. For two years I didn't take a salary. And for those two years, Joe Medina, my bookkeeper and the only one who'd moved up from Temple City with us, worked part-time.

During the time Gail and I were seeing each other once a week, trying to work through our separation, I went ahead and bought a small house in town and moved in. I also took a real estate course and got my license, thinking that I would be buying and selling places for myself. Once again, my intuition was right on.

Among other things, I went to a seminar on financial planning, and learned some things about how to set up a ranch or farm for the best tax benefits. I've always been excited to learn new things. So when I saw an ad for this financial planning course in Los Angeles, I decided to check it out. They had a lot of different aspects of financial planning, including buying precious metals, as well as tax breaks for certain kinds of farming and ranching. During the first day, I remember thinking to myself, well, by golly, I could run a seminar like this in our area. Not that I'd ever done anything like it, but again, nobody told me that I couldn't! I remember that I got really inspired and made notes like mad, trying to grasp as much as I could. I kept my notes, and continued to mull over the idea, because, as I've said before, when you hit on a good idea, you don't just jump into it with both feet right away. You've got to think it through, do the research and talk about it with your friends and acquaintances. Then, after you've given it some long and careful thought, and it still seems like the right thing to do, when the right moment appears, then you jump in. A while later I took Tony and Tiffany to another seminar run by the same guy, this time up at his ranch in Grants Pass, Oregon. I remember coming away thinking to myself, this is a cinch! I know I can do this. During the time that I lived in the little house in town, I kept taking other seminars and related courses, building up my own files with information which I could later present when I launched my own seminars.

It's funny, but I don't recall too much about how Gail and I got back together after our seven months' separation. I guess we just sort of fell back into it. We'd continued seeing each other all throughout the time we were apart. If he wasn't coming up to see me on the weekends, I would be going down to Van Nuys, stopping in on my parents in Temple City, then spending the night with him. I think I told him I wasn't going to wait much longer, and that I'd started to date a little bit. We finally talked, and talked, and in the end, he came back. Like what happened with Woody when we were kids, and he chose a motor scooter over me. I could never fully trust anymore. You never really let yourself go again, for emotional self-protection, I guess. One thing, that came out of the separation though, was the realization that if we were going to stay together and make a go of it, we definitely shouldn't be in business together.

With that in mind, Gail moved into my little house on 2nd Street. But instead of coming back to work with me at Artis, Inc., he went and got work at the Santa Ynez Airport, not too far from where we were living. It was good for him. Aviation was his first love. And it was good for me, since we weren't in each other's hair all the time. Gail decided to give his 49% of the stock in Artis/Aleene, Inc., to the kids, since he was no longer directly involved in the company. We kept him on as a consultant. So he was earning money from that, in addition to his income from the airport.

*

Along with my real estate license, came the "book," the bible of properties on the market in my immediate area. And in that book, I noticed a ranch for sale on Refugio that piqued my interest. I went to check it out, and was intrigued. It was really charming, special, and I knew immediately that this was the place I'd been looking for. It had 6.9 beautiful acres, and three different buildings on it. The front house dated back to the 1920s. Then, there was a little house off to the side called the Casita, and the main house in the back.

We all moved to the property in September, 1981. Tiffany, who was now living near us in Buellton, moved into the old house in the front. Tony took over the Casita. And Gail and I moved into the main house, which was a lot like a Swiss chalet, in the back. There was a swimming pool around which the buildings were arranged. The property also came with barns and eight different pastures for our horses. I gave it the name Tialto Family Farms, after Tiffany,

Aleene, and Tony.

With Tialto Farm, I felt a renewal, both in my personal life and in business. At our new ranch, we all worked like the dickens to fix it up, to make it ours. We had four or five horses at any given time, sheep, rabbits, and even a longhorn steer. Tony took care of the rabbits, while Tiffany tended the sheep. I put in fencing for the horses, (about $30,000 worth!), and a whole bunch of other things, too. I had learned from the seminar I took that you could take a tax advantage if your farm was a business. Later, we added some exotic cats and other animals that we would raise to sell. And it wasn't long after we'd bought Tialto Farm and were moved in, that I actually hosted the first of our own three-day seminars at our new ranch.

My new living room, which was between the kitchen and a bar-type area, could seat 40 people comfortably. I advertised our family farm seminars in the Wall Street Journal. And people came from all over southern California, places like Newbury Park, Arcadia, Torrance, Simi Valley,

The original ranch house at Tialto Family Farms,
originally occupied by Tiffany, then Tony.

Aleene's "Swiss Chalet." Built as a dance and music studio for the original owner of the house. This was the scene of a lot of the original "Aleene's Creative Living" Television Show.

Thousand Oaks, Pacific Palisades, Yorba Linda, Valencia, and even from as far north as Fresno. Generally, all the spaces were taken for our seminars. As I recall, we charged around $200 for the three days, which included a great barbecue. Our participants stayed in a hotel nearby.

We had four or five horses then, plus sheep, rabbits, and a few other things that we discussed at our seminars. The first day, we talked about self-sufficiency; what kind of trees you could buy that were fast-growing so you'd always have firewood, how to smoke fish, and things like that. We outlined for our participants what a person had to do if he or she had a ranch, no matter what the size, tiny or big, to qualify for tax benefits. If it was a real small ranch, you needed to go into something small, like a special breed of rabbit, for example. If it was a great big ranch, you could go into longhorn cattle or llamas or animals of that nature. The main point was that you had to develop a kind of animal husbandry business that was out of the ordinary. For instance, you couldn't go into regular cattle ranching, because it was a well-known fact that in California you couldn't make any profit. But you could go into longhorns, because they sold for a lot more than regular cattle, and there was always profit possibility. Llamas were another good idea, as were ostriches. You could go into Arabian horses if you had a lot of money, but you had to be in the million dollar-and-up category to have any possibility of it being a successful business in the tax agency's opinion. You couldn't just be an average person whose daughter wanted to keep a horse. At our seminars, we also brought in professional speakers, including an accountant to explain the tax advantages and pitfalls, and an attorney to talk about the legal aspects of how to set it up. One of the people who came was a gentleman who is now in the next town up here. He's a TV producer, who bought zebra and other exotic animals. I also had a wildlife specialist come in and give a talk. At that time I had cats, wildcats. I had caracals, a type of lynx found mainly in Asia, and servals, which are very rare in the U.S. As part of the seminars, I also took the people around to visit other farms and ranches in the area. They could talk

"Max" was one of our exotic cats, a serval that we were raising for our tax shelter seminar at Tialto Family Farms. In addition we had horses, rabbits, sheep, longhorn and other types of animals.

with people who were raising llamas, longhorns or whatever was of particular interest to the people who'd come to our seminars. Although the seminars broke even, I did it mainly for fun, and it certainly was!

It was at our wonderful Tialto Family Farms that I started the current television show, "Aleene's Creative Living With Crafts." It first aired on the Lifetime Channel, and is now on The Nashville Network five mornings per week. We shot everywhere. I remember one time the crew even got on top of our old-fashioned water tower to get just the right angle down onto our front porch. During the time they were shooting, I took my bed out of my bedroom, and we used that as the kids' crafts room. It had bookcases and was a really nice location to hang designs. The television crew shot in the kitchen, in Tony's house, out by the pool, the gazebo and the hot tub. Doing the show at Tialto Farm was a lot of fun. There were so many great scenes. We had gates out front, and the beginning of the show had the gates opening. Then the camera went down the driveway which was lined solid with roses for almost the length of a city block! It was ideal, in every sense of the word, and I got many letters from viewers who agreed with me.

*

After we'd gotten back together, Gail went into business as an FBO, Fixed Base Operator, as they call them, at the Santa Ynez Airport, in partnership with a gal named Shy Smith. About a year-and-a-half later, they suddenly lost the contract when the county decided again to put it out for bid.

For a short time, Gail came to work at Artis, Inc., however, he wasn't working in the business itself. Instead, he took over running our machine shop; though that only lasted about four months. The people out at the airport liked Gail so much, that they raised cane about him and Shy losing the contract. A company called Santa Barbara Aviation had won the right to operate the maintenance at the airport. But because the people who used the airport caused such a ruckus, the company just turned around and hired Gail to handle the maintenance. He was great at working on private aircraft, because he loved aviation so much. Sometimes he'd let people work on their own planes, then he'd check over what they'd done to make sure it passed inspection. Though he barely made any money at all doing it, I know it was a fun place for him to work. Gail used to give me some money every month toward his share of food and expenses. But it didn't bother me that he wasn't making money, because I knew he was happy there, doing what he really wanted to do with his life.

*

For a period of about five years after we'd gotten back together, I traveled a lot doing shows all over the country. Gail was at the airport quite a bit, both for meetings at night, and at the workshop during the day. On Saturdays and Sundays, those were the busiest times, he had to be there. He was on call, too. So every time someone had a flat tire, he had to run out to the airport to fix it. Even though we lived under the same roof, we weren't seeing each other too much. After talking about it, Gail decided he would bring in a partner for his Fixed Base Operations; someone to work with him and handle half the load. Gail made contact with a fellow from Alaska who was qualified, and before long that fellow moved down here and became Gail's partner. Gail had built a large hangar out at the airport which he was going to use for fun, now that his new partner had arrived, and he was able to divide up the responsibilities.

But about two weeks later, when it seemed that Gail finally had things the way he wanted, tragedy struck. On February 21, 1986, Gail suffered a serious airplane accident when a World War I-style triplane he was flying, similar to the Fokker flown by Baron von Richtoven of Germany, the "Red Baron," crashed at the Santa Ynez Airport.

Gail had been working on that plane for about two months, doing maintenance checks and the standard review for its owner, prior to flying it for the first time. An eyewitness to the crash reported that the triplane dipped several times in the air shortly after takeoff. Then it banked to the left and suddenly plunged toward an open field at the end of the runway. He was sixty-two years old at the time, and though he survived the crash, he suffered brain damage when his head hit the metal butt of a gun mounted on the plane.

For a month or so, the doctors didn't tell me how bad it really was. At first, they said he's not going to be able to go back to work repairing and working on airplanes. But they said he'd be okay to travel. I was happy that he'd survived, and was under the mistaken impression that eventually, with rehabilitation and therapy, he'd get back to normal. I even went out and bought a 25-foot recreational vehicle, thinking I'd take him on a nice road trip when he got out of the hospital, because of what the doctors had implied about his condition. But a month later, when he was just getting ready to come out of intensive care, I overhead one nurse telling another that Gail would be lucky if he ever walked again. That was when I realized just how badly injured he really was.

When they moved him into rehabilitation, the doctor there told me that Gail had suffered massive head injuries and that he would never fully recover. Sometimes, when accident victims are younger, their nerve endings will reconnect, according to what the doctor said. But because of his age, the prognosis wasn't good. Gail was able, over time, to re-learn to walk, and to feed himself, but the head injury had damaged the part of the brain which controls short term memory. He had long term memory, which meant he knew how to drive a car, or even fly an airplane, for that matter. But if he had to react quickly to something, he just couldn't do it. At the time, the doctors told me he would be in the hospital for at least a year, and even then, they weren't optimistic about the degree of his recovery. Ultimately, Gail was at the Santa Barbara Rehabilitation Institute for a little more than six months. In that time, they got him walking. But someone still had to tell him what to do next. You had to tell him when to get up, when to sit down, things like that. It was a difficult adjustment for me, as you can imagine, to see this man who'd been so in control of himself and his life, suddenly to be so out of control.

We took him to another rehabilitation hospital in Pomona. This one had several different residential centers, and, as the patient progressed, they moved to another house in the hopes that they could get to the level where they could

SANTA BARBARA NEV

The oldest daily newspaper in Southern California

131st Year—No. 275   C   Four sections   Santa Barbara, Calif., Saturday, Feb. 22, 1986

News-Press photo by BILL GRIGGS

Pilot Gail Eckstein was critically injured Friday in the crash of a World War I airplane replica at the Santa Ynez Airport.

Pilot critically injured in crash

SANTA YNEZ — A 55-year-old pilot-mechanic was reported in critical condition at St. Francis Hospital following the crash of a hand-crafted "Red Baron"-styled German Fokker airplane at Santa Ynez Airport Friday afternoon.

Gail Eckstein, 55, of Santa Ynez, underwent emergency surgery at Santa Ynez Vally Hospital in Solvang before being transferred to St. Francis, local hospital officials said. Surgery was scheduled this morning, officials said.

An eyewitness, student pilot and airport lineboy Mike Sanderson, said the bright red replica of a World War I triplane dipped several times in the air shortly after takeoff and began a bank to the left when the wind apparently turned the plane sharply back toward the runway.

It plunged into an open field beyond the end of the runway about 2 p.m., Sanderson said.

Patty Henry of Santa Ynez Aviation said, "he was taking off . . . flying low, and when he gained altitude the plane took a nose dive and crashed into the ground."

Sanderson said that Eckstein had been working on the plane for about the past two months, performing its annual maintenance check. Sanderson said Eckstein had not yet actually flown the plane following the checkup but had driven it around the taxiway several days ago.

Eckstein, the airport's chief mechanic, was taken to the hospital by car after a paramedics vehicle became bogged down in thick mud, deputies said. County and Solvang City fire units were on the scene but there was no fire

following the crash.

It was not immediately known who built the airplane, how long it had been stored at the airport or who owns it.

The plane resembles one flown during World War I by the legendary Baron Manfred von Richthoven, who was known as "the Red Baron" because of the color of his plane and his killing efficiency.

Federal Aviation Administration officials were on the scene late Friday to begin conducting an investigation, deputies said.

take care of themselves. Unfortunately, Gail never got out of the first house. After six months there, I was told that they'd done all they could for him there, and that we'd have to put him in a center for brain-damaged people, or have full-time, round-the-clock help for him at home. I brought him home a few times in the final weeks he was at the center in Pomona, but quickly realized I wasn't going to be able to handle it. One time while he was home, I was about to drive him into town when I realized that I'd forgotten something in the house. I ran back in, and before I came out, Gail got behind the wheel of the car and took off for town by himself.

After realizing that I wouldn't be able to handle him at home, and on the doctor's recommendation, I took him up to a home for people with brain damage in Santa Rosa. It turned out to be a wonderful place. But even there, they had to give him sedatives to stop the frustration. He'd get frustrated if people didn't do what he wanted them to. Or he'd get frustrated if you tried to get him to do something and he couldn't. It took several experienced professionals who knew what they were doing to manage his condition.

After a number of months, my attorney insisted that I had to officially divorce Gail. Because he'd worked on people's airplanes, I could be liable and responsible for years to come if one his clients had a crash as a result of a mechanical malfunction. Of necessity, Gail's son was appointed his conservator for the divorce proceeding. I believed I was going to get him back after the divorce. And certainly I was going to be financially responsible for him for the rest of his life.

Every day, at the home in Santa Rosa, they would take Gail down to an Alzheimer's center, because the symptoms he had were very similar to the symptoms assosiated with Alzheimer's. However, his son didn't like that place, and felt that I wasn't taking good care of Gail. Gail's son didn't want his father to be on sedatives of any kind. And when he forced the doctors to take Gail off the sedatives, the people in charge said he could no longer stay there. I called him all the time at his new place, and he seemed to like the fact that I was calling. But one day his son asked me not to call any more, saying that it was upsetting to him. His son also made it clear that as Gail's conservator, he would never allow him to come back to live with me.

Brain damage is a very costly condition, so it always amazes me when people don't want to follow the helmet rules for riding motorcycles. I believe in people's civil liberties to do as they choose. But from my experience with Gail's brain injury, and the devastating effect it had on our families, I would tell any motorcycle rider who didn't want to wear a helmet to think twice, or maybe even three or four times, before riding without one.

Unlike most people in this situation, I was really lucky that we had a two million dollar umbrella policy through our company. But believe me, I had to fight the insurance company every step of the way to get them to pay what they were responsible for. When Gail was first at the Rehabilitation Institute in Santa Barbara, the insurance said they didn't have to pay the $20,000 per month because it wasn't a hospital, it was an institute. Can you believe that? The next place we moved him, out to Pomona, was $10,000 a month, and they balked at covering that as well, until my attorney got after them again. By the time we had moved him up to the facility in Santa Rosa, it was costing about $3,000 per month, which I was responsible for.

Gail always said that if he discovered he had a terminal disease, like cancer, that he would take that little airplane of his and fly out over the ocean until it ran out of gas. He never, never wanted to live if he was on life support, or under similar conditions. He had even signed documents years earlier, stating that under no condition was he to be hooked up to life support in a hospital. But his physical condition wasn't bad, and he wasn't on life support systems. It was horrible; knowing how terribly frustated Gail was; seeing the limitations he now had to live with, and the tragic turn his life had taken as a result.

Gail two months before accident.

Guests for the "Creative Living" television show, always enjoyed the several different settings such as the gazebo.

CHAPTER NINE

Money, Kids & More Trouble in Paradise

In 1990, I sold Tialto Family Farms. Although it wasn't easy for me to sell it, I knew there were many reasons why it was the right thing to do. For one thing, we were having a cash flow problem at Artis/Aleene, Inc. There are times when it's best to tighten up, though too often people don't do it. My instinct told me to do just that, and in this case it meant selling the ranch. For another thing, the ranch was very costly, not only in making the payments, but having to keep two people full time to maintain it-- a gardener and a ranchhand. Then, when I thought I had it sold, and had already seen a nice little house in the town of Buellton that I wanted to move into, the sale fell through. A year later, the same people came back to buy the ranch, but by then property wasn't worth as much, and prices in the area had gone downhill across the board. But I said to them that I want exactly what I was asking last year, it's not negotiable, and they agreed. Then I took that money and paid cash for my current home.

Tony was living at Tialto Farms then, and I think he and his wife were kind of unhappy when I decided to sell the ranch. But I was seeing more than the cash problem at Artis/Aleene's, Inc.: with the sale of Tialto Family Farms, I would have a chance to get enough money into the account for Gail to last him through the rest of his life. So I decided that was the best thing to do. Also, I remember deciding that I was going to put myself in a financial position that I would be okay, no matter what happened. It's something that I think people, as they get a older, should do, if and when they get the chance.

Many people have asked if I miss Tialto, because it was absolutely gorgeous-- it was the most beautiful ranch I've ever seen, and many of the people who visited I'm sure would agree. But, believe it or not, I don't miss it. I had lots of wonderful times on that property, but after Gail was gone, it had gotten to be a lot work for me. My younger son, Tony, was of great help on specific problems, such as getting me a new water tower installed when the old one started having problems. He was very good at dealing with some big issues, but he wasn't at the ranch on a day-to-day basis because he had so many outside interests at the same time. And while I have wonderful memories of everything that went on at Tialto Farms, including the many television shows that were taped there I've never been sorry about selling it.

I know I've had incredibly good luck when it comes to houses and property, and I love the little house I'm in now. It's warm and tight, and a very restful place for me. It's funny, but I've always been this way-- every house I've ever lived in was right for me at the time, but when I've moved on, for whatever reason, I've never regretted it.

*

I think I've mentioned that I took over running Artis/Aleene, Inc., even before Gail left me in 1978 to go on his "sabbatical" from our marriage. I knew that he'd gotten unhappy with my criticisms of the way he was running things, and even before our separation, when he left and went down to Van Nuys to continue working for his aviation licenses, we had already agreed that he would be less and less involved with the daily operations of the company, in everybody's best interests. My older son, Fred, who had worked along side Gail and was getting familiar with all aspects of the plant, helped me keep things going when Gail was no longer involved. Before too long, however, Fred took off for Scotland on an antique-buying trip with a friend of his. The trip was to be just for a couple of weeks, but Fred stayed on for a while in Scotland and shortly thereafter got married there. And during this period, my younger son, Tony, who'd learned enough from Gail and from Fred, stepped in to fill the gap.

Tony, who'd worked with me pretty much throughout his childhood, began to assume more and more responsibilities in the years following Gail's accident and subsequent incapacitation. Don't forget that Tony was about thirteen when we first moved up to Santa Ynez, and he was twenty-five in 1986, the year Gail had his big accident. Aside from working with Artis/Aleene, Inc., his other jobs were working part-time at the cattle auction, and at one point, for a ditch-digging company called Ditch Witch. So he really grew up with the family business.

The guy who owned Ditch Witch was amazed at Tony's work ethic. They might have someone call in with a broken part or something, and if it meant driving five hours to a job site, Tony would up and do it without giving it a second thought. That sense of the importance of work was another thing Tony and I always had in common. Like myself, Tony wasn't the kind who went home at five o'clock. He worked at Ditch Witch about six months or so, but then decided to come back to work with us. Other than those two jobs, he'd been with Artis/Aleene, Inc., from childhood. He'd traveled with me on the Crafts Caravan when he was eight years old, had taught classes, and emcee'd the drawings and things like that, wherever we went.

At one point I had trouble from the company who supplied us with gold bottles. I had 100,000 bottles on order, but they didn't deliver them, and didn't deliver them. I called over there, and found out they were in bankruptcy and couldn't get them released. Tony immediately said we'd find another bottle-maker. He started calling all over the place, and at about five in the afternoon we drove down to a company he'd discovered in Simi Valley, near Los Angeles. We went and talked to the fellow who managed the company, and he told us he'd have the gold bottles to us in two weeks. Tony was just naturally very good about that, really resourceful. I remember that he took a horse-trailer down to Simi Valley to pick up the finished bottles.

In those days, Tony and I worked fairly well together. Since I was still mostly focused on promotion, design, and public relations, he got more and more into running the production part of it. Little by little he was trying to take over more and more responsibilities, since by his nature he takes

Aleene, Gail and Tiffany with the famous Aleene's Tacky Glue in a giant mock-up size bottle for trade show.

over, that's just the way he is. I have to say, that in spite of all our scrapes, that's one thing I admire about him. Our TV show kept me busy all the time; making products for the show, lining up talent and sponsors, in addition to my actually appearing on the show. We were taping one week out of every month at first, but it soon increased. So, Tony was really free to run the shop.

A couple of years later, I decided that we needed to have something we could mail to the viewers that would tell them what was available to them. When we were first on TV, we asked people to send a self-addressed stamped envelope for particular instruction sheets. But I had the feeling that the information flew by so fast that they couldn't really catch it. I thought I needed a little something that was printed, telling people what was available on the TV show, that I could send them. So I just started it, a newsletter. And I did it for at least eight months before anybody at the shop was even aware that I was doing it. I just did it. I put it together and had it printed without giving it a second thought. On our TV show, I asked people to send in $2.00 for subscription costs. Then one day, Tony came up to me and said, "We're getting these checks for $2.00, what are they for?"

When we went two days a week on television, the response got a little bigger. Then I started working on the publication, to make it look a little nicer. Eventually, when Tiffany came to join us on the television show, she introduced some new ideas about how it should look and what should be in it. Before too long, I turned it over to her, and she helped develop it into our monthly, *Creative Living Magazine*.

*

I don't remember when I decided that I would begin turning the business over to the kids. But one day, I thought, well, I'm getting older, I don't want to run this business forever, and I don't want to sell to anybody else. If my kids are interested in taking it over, that's fine with me. I'll train them for that. I had no idea that it would be as difficult a process as it's turned out to be. But I still would have done it exactly as I have.

Looking back on it, when my father left me to form the Snowfoam Company, he really stayed away and just let me run my own ship. He still gave me his advice and counsel, for which I was grateful, but he was busy managing his own company, and left me to sink or swim. I think that was probably the healthiest way to do it. But then I'm different than he was, so naturally I've ended up doing it differently. I've stayed involved with our family business for a variety of reasons. I though now, at seventy-two, I'm pulling back further and further to follow other pursuits. But pulling away from Artis/Aleene's, Inc., hasn't been, and isn't easy for me.

When I was completely on my own, I knew enough about budgeting to enable me to survive difficult problems, like the loss of my business to Aurora, as well as the re-building of the business once I got it back. I think my ability to budget is probably my very strongest suit. I can save money, operate on a strict budget, and work with less people when I have to. I always see too much paperwork, too much being done that doesn't pay. To me, that's a serious business problem. But it's also a generational thing, I guess, because I have to say that young people today don't really learn about budgeting until maybe it's too late. They aren't taught the importance of running a business-- or a home, for that matter-- on a budget. That's one thing they certainly don't teach in high schools, but they sure should!

In August, 1992, I sold most of my shares in the company to Tony. I did it because he and I had begun arguing all the time, and frankly, it made me unhappy. I'd been mulling it over for about two years when I finally came to the decision to sell to Tony. But I also insisted that Tony would hire a Chief Financial Officer, or CFO as they're called. I was fervently hoping that a professional financial officer could show Tony how to manage money. Well, we hired several, but they weren't that good to begin with, at least in my mind, and not one of them could get through to Tony.

I guess I was sort of spoiled, too, because of my bookkeeper, Joe Medina, who was with me for over twenty-five years. Joe, a single dad raising ten, well-behaved children, was very, very good at bookkeeping and general accounting. He did everything by hand, in the long ago days before computers. If I called his office needing some fact or figure, he always had the answers in two minutes flat! He could tell me who had placed orders, who I needed to call, or a million other things about the business that he had at his fingertips.

As Joe was getting older, we kept hiring these CFO's who were supposed to make use of his expertise, but who, of course, wouldn't listen to him at all. Eventually, he left us to retire, and then he died very soon after retiring. Joe Medina was so good about money. Compared to him, these guys with sophisticated business degrees still had a lot to learn.

With each of the new financial officers we hired, I would talk to them and tell them Tony had lots of good ideas but didn't know anything about budgeting. It was supposed to be their job to create budgets and to work with Tony, to keep him in line with the budget. I let them know that he had his own mind about things, and that sometimes they would be required to hit him over the head with a two-by-four. I think everyone will agree that money is the biggest problem in a business; getting money to grow on, handling it properly, and using money in such a way that it benefits you rather than putting it in the wrong places and losing it. These are the things that decide who survives and who doesn't.

Unfortunately, these guys didn't understand about not spending money. I saw it getting worse and worse. Many of my arguments fell on deaf ears, or so I felt. Every time we'd fight, which was growing more frequent, Tony would throw up his hands, and declare he was going to quit. Then I'd say I'd quit, and let him run it. Finally I said I'd sell him the stock, and I'll get out because I just wasn't going to fight anymore. Selling my shares to Tony didn't really make any difference to me, because if we kept fighting, the shares wouldn't be worth two cents anyway. If I sold them to Tony, I guess I hoped maybe he'd feel responsible to me the rest of my life, which I think he does, so that in my retirement (if and when, that is), I'd receive money for the rest of my life to live on. So while he officially owns most of my shares now, though I've kept a few, he still is responsible to pay me for them over a period of years.

Bankruptcy came a year or so after I'd sold most of

my stock to Tony, and then the struggles really began.

*

Some people have wondered why I didn't appoint Fred, my older son, to take over. I believe that people have different abilities, and I think you have to guide them into the right job for their skills and interests. For one thing, Fred, who'd gone off to the Coast Guard, and later to Scotland, had left the company twice for extended periods, and so in going and coming back twice, he lost a little ground in the operation. But it still wouldn't have made any difference as to who ended up running the business. I knew Fred understood this, because he never really liked the financial aspects of it. He isn't that type. He doesn't think along those lines. He's very good at what he does. And Fred can do things Tony can't, and vice versa.

And it's the same way with Tiffany and Heidi. They're different in their interests, talents and skills, as it should be. In figuring out how things were going to be run after I pulled back, I had to just take the bull by the horns and say "This is how I see it going." Heidi is excellent in design, but she never wanted to be bothered with running the company. She's very creative. Tiffany was always very well-organized. Heidi was always a little more independent, too, preferring not having anyone over her, while Tiffany had worked under bosses in different positions, and has great people skills. Then, too, Tiffany and Tony worked well together, where as Heidi doesn't work well with him. So each one of my children has their differences, and each contributes to the whole. None of them are alike, and I certainly wouldn't want them to be.

I think a lot of families don't realize the importance of recognizing individual strengths. People ask how the family can get along, working so intensely in business together. Believe me, it isn't easy! We've had times when everybody's mad, and it takes a little while to get over it. Right now I'm mad at Tony, although some of the stuff I fought with him about yesterday, he finally accepted, and is working it into our future plans. But, I had to fight to get him to listen to me. I wish that wasn't so, but I understand to a degree why it is, and I've learned to live with it.

In most companies when a parent turns it over to their kids, the parent usually gets out of the way, retiring, moving on to something else. My father was very smart in that regard. He got out and that was that. And while I keep saying I shouldn't get into these arguments, I can't help myself when I see something that I feel is not in the best interest of the company. I've got to speak up, and some of the time, my speaking up makes waves.

*

In the years following Gail's accident, as I worked to keep the business growing, I developed a close friendship with a man named Barney Pruetting, who was also in our industry. Barney and I became great pals, and being able to talk with him on the phone about business and everything else, was wonderful.

I'd first met Barney many years earlier, but we didn't get to be friends until the day we ran into each other at the airport in Memphis. At the time, I was wrapping up a visit to the company he worked for, Wang, Inc., and was waiting to board a plane, when I felt someone tap me on the shoulder. I turned around as I heard him saying, "I don't think you remember me, but I'm Barney Pruetting, from Wang."

We started chatting and I learned that he had become the assistant to the president of Wang, Inc., whom I had just left after a meeting where I was trying to sell him paint. Since Barney and I were taking the same flight, we sat together on the airplane. I remember that I was traveling with another guy, Stan, who was with the paint manufacturing company, and it turned out that all three of us were on our way to visit the same company in Chicago. When we landed there, Barney asked if I would like to ride with him. I said fine, and let Stan rent the other car.

Barney and I just hit it off. We talked, talked, and talked the whole way. When we got out to the facility, they were having a company barbecue. Barney and I sat together and kept talking about how he liked horses, how I liked horses. He had ridden gaited horses, which is something not many people know about, so it's rare to meet someone who can really talk about it. We parted there, and a couple of weeks later, I got a call from him. We started chatting a lot back and forth on the phone, then meeting for lunch or dinner when we knew we were going to be in the same city on business. I have to say that he was the smartest person I ever met in my life.

Barney's company, Wang's, was a long-time customer of mine. They were also importers. The company was owned by a Chinese-born businessman, Robert Wang, a very unusual gentleman. Another self-made person, he started out living in his truck and traveling around selling macramé cord. Then the business grew and grew. Robert Wang had gone to school in Memphis, and when he was recruiting, he hired Barney who was just out of college and was himself starting out with nothing. Then, Barney was given a territory to sell, and I know he lived in his car, traveling and selling, and over time, he worked his way up the ladder as the company continued to grow.

In those years, Wang, Inc., was probably selling around twelve million dollars annually. Barney moved up until he became sales manager, and after that, marketing and merchandising manager. He was so good at what he did that I'm sure he was being groomed to be president of the company. What made Barney special in our industry was that he had a lot of art ability, but he also had a lot of business ability. And he was really loved by everyone who came in contact with him.

I knew that Barney was gay, and that our friendship would always be platonic, but it was a deep friendship nevertheless because we were able to communicate well on so many different levels. Like me, he had struggled in his life to make a success of himself, nothing had ever been handed to him.

In 1991, Barney and I went on a three-week trip to Europe together. We took the Orient Express, and the experience was nothing less than fantastic. We went to Paris, then took the train to Venice, then another train from Venice to Rome. Barney was one of those people with a great sense of humor, and he kept me laughing during the whole trip.

But a few months after we returned from the trip, in either October or November, 1991, Barney discovered that he had full-blown AIDS, and that the disease was progressing very fast. He quit his job and came out here and stayed with me for a month. We spent a lot of time together and traveled up the beautiful California coast to Carmel for a week. He had such dreams for his life, and had it going so well, that it was heartbreaking to know that he was dying. After Barney had gone home, I got it in my head that I was going to do something special for him. I knew how much he liked my mare, Whoopie Maid, so I arranged for her to be shipped back east to him. I know he rode her for a few months, at least, and that in those remaining weeks she gave him some comfort in that special way that only animals can give us.

Barney Pruetting was such an inspiration to me, because he was both a tremendous business person and so incredibly likable. During my own troubles, as I was trying to figure out how the business might be turned over to my kids, he filled a special place for me, because Barney was somebody I could talk to everyday on the phone-- about cus-

Barney with my Quarter Horse Maire "Whoopie Maid."

Barney and his dog, just before he died.

tomers and business, about my problems and about his-- and still have lots left to talk about.

Barney was so well-liked, that after his death, our industry started an AIDS Auction at the Association of Crafts & Creative Industries, setting up a scholarship in his name. I just really hated to lose him. You see all these horrible people on drugs, wasting their lives, and then you see somebody with such a brilliant mind, such a beautiful soul, brought down by this horrible disease. It's just not right, but it's the way it is.

*

In 1991, at Tony's encouragement, we made plans to set up a small bottling operation in Mexico, in a commercial area not too far from the California border. I had many reservations about moving part of our operation to Mexico, but finally I agreed to it. I told Tony that I only wanted to fill one item down there, our 4-ounce bottles of tacky glue. But Tony, always "thinking big," moved in to Mexico on a much larger scale than I had anticipated. And it turned out to be very, very bad for us.

At the time, we were running out of space at the shop because we were bringing so many things in. It was my thought that if we only moved one part of our operation down there, it could be done in a small space. But gung-ho-Tony decided to do a couple of other size bottles down there as well. Naturally, this required renting a larger building. Soon after, as I recall, we went into yet a larger building. And eventually, we moved into a huge building.

Today, I would tell anybody and everybody who wants to listen: Never do business in Mexico! As business-people, they're less than honest, and they're so behind in basic commercial necessities, like telephones and electricity, installation of which is terrible in Mexico. Everything seems dirty, yet when you go down there, talking about possibly setting up a business, they're only too happy to show you a few commercial plants that look really good. For example, they showed us a medical supply company's warehouse that was supposedly spotless. Well, in one way it was, but to my thinking, it didn't really measure up. It seems to me that their workers aren't really trained in the basics, generally speaking, and they aren't knowledgeable in a lot of areas.

It was so bad, that Fred had to spend most of his time in Mexico managing the operation, and that was really tough. He'd drive down early Monday mornings, leaving at 4 a.m. or so, get there by 10 a.m., then come back on Friday evenings. But managing a company long distance doesn't work. For a while there, we didn't realize stuff was being stolen out of our plant, which was really stupid! When you send down a drum you expect to get back x-number of cases of bottled glue. But there were too many times when we were expecting to get 50 cases back, but only got 35, and nobody noticed it. Instead of really following through at the plant up here, they just assumed the other 15 cases were going to come on another truck. We probably went four or five months before discovering it was anywhere between $225,000 to $250,000 worth of merchandise that was missing.

On top of it all, when we finally knew we had to throw in the towel, we had trouble getting out of our contract with the Mexican company that we'd been working with. In fact, we had to get out of it through bankruptcy. By that time, the Bankruptcy Court had jurisdiction over it because the company we were working with was in San Diego. And, in the end, we had a horrible time getting our machinery out of Mexico. Don't say I didn't warn you!

*

Another of Tony's mistakes centered around a jewelry manufacturing company. One day, a guy came by and wanted to rent one of our buildings which was off to the side of our main location. This man intrigued Tony with the idea that there was a lot of money to be made in jewelry manufacturing. Before too long, Tony was convinced that we should get into it. Unfortunately, Tony never really discussed it with the rest of the family, and actually negotiated the deal without telling us. He came to us after the deal was already done, and presented it to the other shareholders, Fred, Heidi, Tiffany, Candy and me. He doesn't remember it that way, of course, but that's the way I remember it happening.

The way Tony recalls it, we had a meeting and discussed it, with the opportunity to approve or not. But he fed us information that wasn't quite so, through no fault of his own. This guy had said he had orders for $100,000 and up, and he made all kinds of other claims, which turned out to be just that, claims. Tony believed him and set it up in our building, which meant he had to build a lot of stuff and spend a lot of money to move this jewelry company in. In addition, he spent money to maintain the jewelry company's sales office in Los Angeles, as well as other costs that were never talked about in the original negotiations. According to the terms of the deal, we also took responsibility for all expenses and for all new purchases, as well as paying the guy a really high salary. This annoyed me no end, because normally with a salesperson, you go with a commission basis and a low salary. After a short while, it became clear that it wasn't working.

I was unhappy because right from the beginning I could feel it wasn't going to work. I didn't like the guy; especially when two months went by and I didn't see any figures.

He hadn't sold one penny, absolutely no sales for one month. I don't where he was, or what he was doing. Even he didn't know he hadn't made any sales for a whole month, and Tony certainly didn't know. Finally, I told Tony I wanted to drop it. Give it to the guy, I don't care what you do, I don't want it. I don't know how it came about, but Tony asked to buy out the contract himself, and I said that was fine. In the end, Tony bought it for $100,000 or something. We were already into some $400,000 in expenditures, though Tony says it was $200,000.

I don't recall this gentleman's salary, but in my mind it was too large. This made me angry, and it was something that really upset the other kids, too. They felt as part-owners that they deserved a say in the board meetings. But at the time, Tony didn't have board meetings. He wasn't sharing information with the other owners. At that time he owned a little bit more shares than the rest of the kids. Fred also owned a little bit more. Candy owned the least amount because, living back east, she wasn't actively involved with the company. But, at the time, I still had the controlling interest in it.

We kept fighting over this jewelry fiasco, it seems, for months. Tony kept walking out, then I'd walk out. Finally, I said "This is silly, I don't want the company in my old age." I told Tony I'd turn it over to him, but he'd have to buy it at book value.

In a lot of ways, I blame myself for Tony's not really understanding the value of money for so long, and I think it's been true of my other kids too, with the exception of Candy. I also think it's something that has happened across the board in this country, starting in the early 1960s, when kids were growing up and there was a lot of money in the country. They never had a chance to learn the value of it. But the pendulum has swung back the other way, unfortunately or not, since the economy started heading south in the 1980s.

Then, too, I financed so much of what Tony did when he went into real estate deals. An acquaintance of ours had bought some property up in the town of Nipomo, not far from where we live, and he made a fortune, which I know inspired Tony. This gentleman was also in the crafts field and had a business making frames. Tony saw him earning a lot of money in real estate, so my son got me to go in on some property with him. Our first try did very well, and made some money. We took that and put it into a second venture with this other guy, but he absconded with the funds. I finally had to sue him, but I got that money back, though it took me three or four years.

At one point, Tony also got investment money from some other people he had talked into coming in with him. Unfortunately, the deal turned sour, but it seemed to me that he didn't feel any responsibility for it, something I couldn't understand. Then I helped him out in a few other situations which also ended up losing me money. He was going in with a group of people in nearby Lompoc, investing in an apartment building and other properties. When one of the guys backed out at the last minute, Tony and the other people would have lost their money, so I invested with him at the last minute, to help him out. Again, it ended up that I lost money. His in-laws were even involved in it. I remember that I repaid them money just to get out. In a sense, I guess I really spoiled Tony. So I was surprised later, when the bankruptcy came up and he felt responsible. In fact, Tony took responsibility, really took charge in the battle to get us out of bankruptcy.

As I'm writing this, I'm realizing that my kids have really come along fine. I know that my continuing involvement as a consultant with the company makes things a little confusing for all of us, while they are taking over more and more. I'm sure that a lot of what I've said or done in the past year or two has been annoying to them in their efforts to successfully manage things. And who knows, quite often they're right about things that I think they are wrong about. Perhaps it will turn out right for them, even though I would have done it another way. As I've said, when my father separated from our original company and started Snowfoam, he didn't bother me at all. In fact, if I needed help, I had to go and ask him, though of course I tried my best not to. Otherwise, he just stayed away and let me do my own thing. In a way, I'd love to be able to do that. But my life has been so intricately involved with my business for so many years, that "retiring" from it is something I'm groping my way through, trying to figure out how to disengage myself in the right way.

I know that Tony has learned a lot through our recent troubles, and grown a lot, too, though like all of us, he still has much to learn. But I don't think he's going to learn it as long as I keep bitching. And I can't help it when I go to a meeting and see something happening that I think isn't right. Both Tiffany and Tony knew I was mad this week, but then I thought, this is stupid. I don't need it. I don't need to be mad. I know I've got to stay away from the meetings, because for so many years I was in charge, I was the one making the decisions, and it's almost impossible for me to see someone else making the decisions when I think they're wrong.

CHAPTER TEN

Battle of the Bankruptcy

When we finally realized we would have to declare bankruptcy, late in 1993, none of our consumers or television viewers out there had any idea that Artis/Aleene's, Inc., was having financial difficulties. To someone looking at us from the outside, we looked good. Our company had close to 100 employees at the time, with more at our plant down in Mexico. We'd been in business almost fifty years, and our magazine circulation was up around 26,000 a month. Our television show, which had been on the air in one form or another for about seven years, was getting more and more popular. And Aleene's Tacky Glue and our other products were still selling well. As far as the public knew, everything was fine.

But we knew that wasn't the case, and internally, we were all going through hell, both emotionally and financially. Sure, we all felt that Tony was in great measure responsible for a lot of what had gotten us into trouble, but looking back on it now, I realize that I should have been more active in putting on the breaks to some of what happened. Fortunately, I'm happy to be able to tell you that Tony shouldered most of the effort to save our ship, when many thought it was sinking. And in the process, he got quite an education, about business, about budgeting, and a world of other things, too, I was responsible for the cash problem because of my insistence on keeping our T.V. Show. The cost of producing the T.V. Show was considerably more than we could afford, but I felt it necessary for promotion for the future.

In the preceding chapter, I gave you some of the details of how we'd started getting into trouble. Looking back on it now, I see that our problems began when we didn't stay focused on what we did really well. We branched out too much. We got all these ideas, and we tried to do them all at once because we knew there was a need for them, but we just shouldn't have branched out like that. For example, Tony would say, Let's package glitter. Well, that sounded good. Or, Let's do some rubber stamps, and that sounded good, too. We were doing some wood products down in Mexico, and someone would come to us and say: You're producing wood products, why don't you do some plaques for us? So all of a sudden we found ourselves further into the wood business. But the wood business in California has all kinds of regulatory restrictions, making it almost impossible to paint or finish wood items within the state. So when we got into wood, some of it had to be done here, some of it in Mexico. And that project in turn caused us to have to re-do one of the buildings we owned, and again the expenses started to mount, as they did with all the different ventures we got into.

I think I mentioned that we hired several chief financial officers, and finally got one who seemed to know his stuff, but he never could get through to Tony. I told him when I hired him that Tony has budgeting problems. Tony can talk anyone into anything, and he kept saying: Oh, next month's going to be a big month, and so they budgeted accordingly, believing their own projection. And I said: No, no, no-- don't budget by what you're hoping will happen next month, budget from what actually happened last month. If it was a bad month, then budget even less. Don't just hope or assume it's going to be a better month. But Tony refused to see it from that perspective, and so he had to learn the hard way.

When we first began discussions about the bankruptcy, the legion of attorneys and the banks involved with our problems wanted me to take back ownership of the shares in the company which I'd sold to Tony. According to their way of thinking, the whole business was going to go down the tubes if I didn't officially take back the shares, and since Tony hadn't fully paid me for them, I was legally entitled to do so. But I refused.

At the time all this was unfolding, I was approaching

seventy years old, (though of course I felt like I was in my mid-forties!), and I said, well, if it fails, it fails. I've got a lot of other things I can do and want to do, and anyway, I didn't want to run it any more. I wanted Tony and the kids to take it over completely and run it successfully, with myself advising and doing some of it as needed. But if I took back those shares from Tony, it would be going backwards, it seemed to me, and I said no, Tony's going to do or die with it. The attorneys and the banks were all after me, but I stuck to my guns. And I have to say, Tony did a really great job of pulling us through it. We tightened up wherever possible, at one point laying off some 60 employees, though as things got better we hired many of them back. All of us took substantial pay cuts, as well, to keep costs to a minimum.

I still own a small number of shares, the same as what the other kids own, but I felt that since he was the one who was going to lead it if anything happened to me, he should own the bulk of the shares. The kids were all very unhappy with him as we went into the bankruptcy, but in the three years since all this happened, Tony has gotten their confidence back because he showed that he really had the ability to pull the company through this awful situation. And Tony and I were pretty much in agreement as the bankruptcy battle raged on. He was handling it very well, much better than I could have, had I been so inclined. I was so mad at attorneys in general, that I just threw up my hands and said: You guys go ahead and deal with it, and see what you all come up with, I really don't care. I don't know how Tony took all of that negativity and wrestled with it, but he did.

Another thing that I'm proud about is how our employees stuck with us through the difficulties of the bankruptcy proceedings. They didn't flee the ship, the supposedly "sinking" ship. The people we had running different parts of our operation stayed with us, which really was amazing. Despite all the things that happened, they had enough trust to stay with us, to trust the fact that we were going to pull through it. I have to give a lot of credit to our employees, but in some ways, it's also a credit to us. We had to have established something good to begin with to have the confidence of the employees to stay with us, and not say, Oh boy, we're gonna be out of a job soon, we're better start looking for something else! And they all had to work real long hours in many cases, to put together information that we needed for bankruptcy Court. The CFO that I'd some doubts about, showed his worth and worked day and night as we progressed through the torturous twists and turns of the bankruptcy proceedings.

Talk about records! When you're going into bankruptcy, you have to change your bookkeeping because they have a trustee in bankruptcy to whom you have to report. The trustee wants the documents one way, the lawyers want them another way, and then you've got a creditors' committee who wants it yet another way! Right now, I've got about eight boxes in my office full of documents from the bankruptcy, and that's not even all of it, either, because everything had to be copied from all the many parties involved, so reams and reams of paper resulted from these proceedings, and I'm sure they used up a small forest in paper on our case alone!

*

As we were experiencing more problems in late 1993, in one of those special coincidences, it happened that my older daughter, Candy, back east, had been at a dinner with her husband, Ed, whose business involves food brokering, and one of the dinner guests was from what they call a "turn-around" company, people who specialize in helping companies like ours when they're in trouble. Something was mentioned about Artis/Aleene's, Inc., having financial problems or something along those lines, and so Candy connected us to this company called Buccino and Associates, based in Illinois.

A few days later, a representative called us from their Los Angeles office, and after talking with him on the phone, we had him come up to Buellton to help us review our situation. It turned out he was very, very good for us. In some ways, he probably over-did it, but money-wise he was just what Tony needed. This gentleman from Buccino put up a large chalkboard with all our company's figures on it divided in segments, showing Tony what he'd done over the past year or so, and where he'd gone wrong. You have to get productivity out of Mexico, he told Tony, and you have to close up the wood shop, which we did. You've got to cut back here, trim down there, you've got to do this, got to do that. Finally, Tony understood how bad the situation really was. At the end of two months of consultation with the Buccino Company's representative, it was his conclusion that we hire a bankruptcy attorney as soon as possible.

The advisor from Buccino suggested two different lawyers who specialized in bankruptcy, and one of them, who we were interested in, came out from Omaha, Nebraska. His company had an office in Los Angeles, but he was based in Omaha. He was a very, very interesting guy, in that he had been involved in re-writing the bankruptcy laws some years back, and he was the attorney that we finally chose to help us.

This man was very knowledgeable, and told us when he came out that it would cost us about $50,000 for bankruptcy proceedings, but it ended up costing well over a million-and-a-half dollars, all told! It wasn't all his fault that he gave us such a low figure coming in, because he didn't have any idea what our problems were, or what had been transpiring throughout the preceding two years. I remember that it amazed him that there were about six different people or companies trying hostile takeovers of Artis/Aleene's, Inc. That alone ended up costing us a lot of money, because he had to keep fighting them off. But overall, the arrival of Buccino's representative and this lawyer, was very good, because these people taught Tony how to budget, and how to move around in the legal maze.

We met with the Omaha attorney for about two months, as I recall, because at that time yet another company was interested in buying us out. Our newly-hired bankruptcy attorney wasn't so sure we had to go into bankruptcy, since that other company was waiting in the wings to buy us. I wasn't too happy about the tack this attorney took at different times, and we fought throughout the whole thing. At one point I seriously wanted a different attorney, but I couldn't get one because one of the banks involved, our bank, wouldn't give us permission to pay another lawyer some money in advance. You couldn't retain another attorney without a downpayment in advance, and in this instance the bank was controlling the money. I have to say that the banks were really uncooperative throughout the whole thing, they were just firmly against anything that we did or proposed to work out our problems.

When we finally got through it all, we had to pay the three different attorneys that were bankruptcy specialists-- a senior bankruptcy attorney, a junior bankruptcy attorney, and a business bankruptcy attorney. The main lawyer got around $375 an hour, although, thankfully, he didn't charge us to come out from Omaha because he had an L.A. office. In actuality, we had four attorneys, because we had the L.A. office attorney from his office, and then we had the business guy from Buccino and his boss, and then we had to pay the creditors attorney throughout this whole thing. We also had to pay Union Bank's attorney, because when you enter into bankruptcy you promise that if you go into litigation you will pay the costs.

At the time, we had several equipment leases, like a lease on our million dollar printing press, among others. They had a slew of attorneys, and, to my way of seeing, they were all nasty. In most cases, we didn't miss a payment. In fact, one we did miss was to Bank of America, on our building, but we were willing to pay it since we had the money in the bank. But then our bank wouldn't let us pay the Bank of America. The bank said that because our Bank of America loan was on the building, and we didn't owe a whole lot of money on it, there was enough equity backing it in case everything fell apart. So they didn't let us pay on it. Everything that we owed Bank of America, even in the bank loan that we had then, they could have sold and gotten money out of it. Bank of America's attorney fought with everyone and caused a major fight on all levels.

At first, I had Mr. Emil Steck as my personal counsel. He's the lawyer I've had for thirty years, the one who successfully got me out of the Aurora deal when everyone told me it was impossible, who was both my corporate attorney and my personal attorney. But he couldn't play both those roles in the bankruptcy, so this bankruptcy specialist from Omaha said: Well, you should have him as your corporate attorney, and then you should get another personal attorney, because on some of the leases you have signed personal guarantees. You're going to need a really good attorney if something happens on your personal guarantees, he insisted.

So he gave us the name of someone who he said was really good, and I contacted him. That lawyer asked for a $10,000 retainer, which I immediately sent him, only it turned out that his license had been suspended by the California Bar Association! And my Omaha attorney, who'd recommended the man, had no idea he'd been suspended! Mr. Steck was the one who found out this fellow had been suspended, otherwise I would never have known it. And I never got that $10,000 back, either.

So much depends on which attorney you have. Mr. Steck is really from the "old school," i.e. a school where they have ethics and integrity. Unfortunately, I know he's going to retire before too long, but, oh boy, do I hate to lose him! He is absolutely fantastic. So I guess there's at least one good attorney out there. I think at one time attorneys probably were honest and good people, but nowadays, I really feel like a lot of the ills of the United States can be placed squarely at the feet of the brotherhood of attorneys.

*

Throughout this period of close to three years, while Tony and the other kids were fighting and wrestling with bankruptcy proceedings, our business kept running, and my job continued to be keeping our customers happy, keeping in touch with them, with the vendors, and also staying in touch with the creditors' committee.

Part of my education in all of this was realizing that bankruptcy laws aren't made to protect the company that's in trouble, like ours was. From my firsthand experience, these laws only benefit the attorneys. And, of course, attorneys make the laws. I originally thought that bankruptcy laws were made for a company to have a breathing period. But you don't. You're supposed to have a certain number of months during which no other company can come in with a hostile takeover attempt. And yet, it seems to me, they still let people come in with hostile takeover attempts.

By now, I'm convinced that the bankruptcy laws

aren't planned for anybody but the attorneys. Generally, the attorney gets paid first, at the end of the bankruptcy. Consequently, since they saw that we were having trouble, they wanted us to sell to anybody who wanted us-- so that they, the attorneys, would be sure to get their money. We started having all kinds of hostile takeover tries, which meant that we had our attorneys continually battling those companies trying to take us over. These hostile companies, for their part, wanted to come in and look at our books. They wanted to go through everything, find out who we were selling to and private information like that, which we didn't want to let them have. So there was a continual battle in court about that.

And, as I've said, bankruptcy is not what it's supposed to be. It's not for the benefit of trying to keep a company in business so that they don't have to lay off their people. And it's not really to the benefit of the vendors who are owed money. It's only to the benefit of the attorneys, really. there is little, if any, incentive for all of the lawyers to rush and settle a case. The more they fight, the more they make. If you survive it, you're lucky just to get through it. Nine times out of ten, the people who take the biggest beating are the vendors, the suppliers. We have two or three bankruptcies against us right now--companies we've been selling to who've gone into bankruptcy, and in most cases, they're not paying us anything on their due bills. They're giving us stock in a new company--not much stock, at that, and it's not worth anything to you. But that's what's happening, so we, having sold them glue, aren't getting anything from it except we still keep them as customers. To me, this is important, probably the most important thing of all. .

When another company tries to come in and take you over, they offer a competitive plan to the creditors committee whereby they will take over the debts and pay people off at a certain rate. The creditors committee, which represents the companies who are owed, and the judge say, gee, the creditors are going to be paid off and all, sounds good to us, what's the deal? But in our case, every one of the takeover companies wanted me to go with them, and I wouldn't. They wouldn't take the company without me, and I had to fight with them all the time.

One of these various takeover attempts came in the form of a businessman who really resembled a large, very hungry shark. He was a gentleman who had been working with the bankruptcy of yet another company. He had some decent ideas about how our problem might be worked out, and was able to come up with a plan, but ultimately the very company he was representing went into Chapter 7, another form of bankruptcy. About a day or two before, he had presented his plan to our creditors' committee and everybody was in pretty much in agreement. Then he suddenly came up with two or three things that I couldn't live with, so I turned his deal down.

After these negotiations started falling through, a friend of mine who owned another craft company got in touch with us about possibly helping out. We talked and talked, and pretty soon it looked like a reasonable deal could be made with them, and it looked like everybody was going to be happy about it. I was happy because I could work with him--I knew him from the past and had always found him trustworthy and honorable. Their attorney had been working on it and came into court on a Friday and told us that everything looked fine, and that they were going to pay everybody off, cash and everything. Then came Monday morning, and out of the blue they announced they were backing out. And I never did really know why. When this company backed out on us, the creditors' committee started getting kind of tired of the lengthy process. What was more disheartening was that we had only one week to go before a court hearing, and now we were back at ground zero!

When the negotiations with these different companies would fall through, it was usually because there some-thing in their proposals that we couldn't accept, and in most cases it centered around me personally-- binding me up in a contract so that I couldn't engage in other pursuits, whether it was television or publishing, that kind of thing.

We always knew that Artis/Aleene's, Inc., could eas-ily be sold to a larger concern. Over the years, many people had wanted the name Aleene's, which I'd been building up for nearly half a century, and they were willing to buy the company from us just to get it. I guess they thought that, for some reason or another, once you got the name, everything else was grand, which it's not. There's a heck of a lot more to a business than the name, though of course the name is quite important. So we talked to a few different companies who were very interested in acquiring us, just to see what our options might be. Prior to filing bankruptcy, our advisors told us to do anything to avoid it, including the outright sale of the company. We negotiated with a company that was fully in agreement to letting me keep the rights to the use of the name Aleene's, which was what I wanted. Under their original terms, I could have kept the name to license to other companies and other products. So we negotiated a bit with them.

After a number of meetings, and as things were getting more difficult in our finance department, we finally reached an agreement. Everyone met for two full days with my regular attorney, my bankruptcy attorney, the business bankruptcy attorney, the Buccino Company representative, their bankruptcy attorney, all of us sitting in one very packed room.

It seemed to me that everything was fine, a deal had been struck, and so I didn't even go to the meeting on Sunday because it was supposed to be finalized. Then their attorney changed the ballgame. Now the deal was off. This was our last hope before filing bankruptcy. Suddenly our attorney was saying, You've got to file bankruptcy. It's got to be done this week, because you've got a problem now that there's no deal.

So four days later, they marched in and filed bankruptcy, under Chapter 11. When you do that, you're assigned a number, which means then that you are protected in bankruptcy court, and the people you do business with get paid-- from that point on. They don't get the money you owed them from before the filing, but from then on they are guaranteed to get some money.   It happened that the creditors' committee had on it our top five suppliers, the people who provided us with the glue resins and stuff, people who were really supporters of ours, as well as my bottle guy, who was also very good with me. But the creditors' committee represented all the creditors, and we had two or three hostile creditors as well as the ones who were our supporters. We had one guy that did our racks for us that was very hostile. It was really a stupid position for him to take, because, you know, in the long run he lost our business, since we had to go someplace else for the racks.

But boy, I'll tell you that the creditors' committee attorney made me mad several times. I think I'm finally getting over it a little bit. But all the attorneys seemed to make it harder. Of course, when you look back on it, maybe it had to be that hard in order to make an impression on us. We had to have that much trouble. If it had been easy, we wouldn't have learned enough. In retrospect, it had to be hard.

Then, after we filed, I began to call my customers all over the country, and ask them to pay some or all of their current orders in advance. This would give us an immediate infusion of capital to run the business with. The various attorneys and the business consultants all said not to bother, it would never happen. Businesses that are used to paying 30 or 60 days after their orders would never pay in advance.

I started calling around to my customers, and you know what? They all said they'd put up something, if not the whole amount! In the next two days, I raised $400,000 dollars in advance payments on orders! Everyone was very surprised. The attorneys couldn't believe it. In fact, the woman bankruptcy court judge couldn't believe it. When she heard what had happened, she asked me in court, What in the world is this tacky glue that these customers would do this for you?

The next day, while the bankruptcy proceedings were going on, we sent money down to our glue people, our bottle people, and several other suppliers who were waiting for payment. Now, in spite of everything that was going on with the legal eagles, we were able to package products and get it out to our customers.

In bankruptcies, you're usually supposed to pay the attorneys off right at the end of bankruptcy, on the date the court sets. But they all agreed to three payments over three months. From the beginning, we felt it was important to pay our total debt off to all our creditors. Now all the attorneys are paid off, and we've paid a large amount off to the vendors. We have two more thirds to pay over the next couple of years. You're still under bankruptcy protection until everybody is paid in this case.

It's been a really interesting experience for me, and all I can say is if a person is an attorney, a lawyer, do not vote them into office because, you know, everybody now has seen what's happened since lawyers have been running this country. From the O.J. Simpson "Trial Of the Century," to the lady who got millions because she spilled hot coffee on herself at McDonald's, the world as defined by lawyers has gone absolutely insane.

But throughout the bankruptcy, Tony saw that I kept my promises, that if I made a promise to somebody, I stuck to it. I know the bankruptcy has been a hard lesson for Tony and for all of us, but it's also been a really good lesson. For the rest of his life he's not going to want to go through that again. I think he realized that once you're the head of a company, where do you go to work if you lose the company?

The whole bankruptcy period lasted about twenty months, from November, 1993, through July, 1995. I'm happy to be able to report that now, as I write this in the spring of 1996, we've recovered from that near-fatal catastrophe, and things are going great guns. We've increased our consumer services department to forty-five people, and today we get anywhere between 3,000 to 5,000 calls a day from customers who are placing orders or wanting information about our craft-related products. Our monthly magazine, Creative Living With Crafts, now published by Oxmoor House, a division of Time-Warner, is up to around 160,000 circulation, and our television show has expanded to a full hour, instead of the half-hour we had before.

Recently, the Santa Barbara News-Press did a major story on us "bouncing back from hard times," written by one of their business reporters, Mark Van De Kamp, in which he had a quote I especially like, from one of the trustees in U.S. Bankruptcy Court in Los Angeles:

"It's very unusual for a company to get through the Chapter 11 process this quickly, and to pay off 100 percent," said Marjorie Lakin Erickson, an assistant trustee in U.S. Bankruptcy Court in Los Angeles. "Less than 5 percent of companies entering Chapter 11 ever complete the process and their payment plan."

Artis, Inc. 85 Industrial Way 1996
This is the Aleene's Division of Artis Inc. as it looks today. Though we
had added on to the original building, because of Santa Barbara County,
we were unable to add additional space needed, so we moved a portion
of our manufacturing to Mexico. Disaster. We are now out of Mexico.
Some of our filling has been subcontracted to a company in Fresno,
California.

Artis Inc. bounces back from hard times

The Buellton-based household crafts company came out of Chapter 11 in July and appears stronger than ever.

By MARK VAN DE KAMP
NEWS-PRESS STAFF WRITER

Artis Inc., a Buellton-based multimedia company devoted to household crafts, is emerging from the most difficult chapter in its history.

Known to millions for its best-selling product — Aleene's Original Tacky Glue — Artis is stronger and wiser after 20 months reorganizing under Chapter 11 bankruptcy protection — from November 1993 to July 1995, its executives say.

Production and employment are at high levels again. By mid-1998 the company plans to pay the last of four $800,000 annual payments to creditors to repay 100 percent of debt, said president Tony Hershman and founder Aleene Jackson.

"It's very unusual for a company to get through the Chapter 11 process this quickly, and to pay off 100 percent," said Marjorie Lakin Erickson, an assistant trustee in U.S. Bankruptcy Court in Los Angeles.

"Less than 5 percent of companies entering Chapter 11 ever complete the process and their payment plan."

Climbing out of the red wasn't easy, Hershman and Jackson said. It took a team effort, some luck and $1.5 million in lawyer and consultant fees that ate up two years of profits.

The company also fought off several hostile takeover efforts during those 20 months, successfully convincing the court and creditors to go with its deal, Hersh-

Company president Tony Hershman and founder Aleene Jackson have brought Artis Inc. back from the brink of extinction.

man said.

"For a while, we were in crisis and laid off 60 of our 95 employees," Hershman said. "Now, we've turned things around and we're very optimistic that we're going to have the most profitable year in our history."

Artis currently has a workforce of 135, including 100 on a full-time basis, making it the second-largest employer in Buellton. Most of its staff members live in Lompoc.

Founded 47 years ago by Aleene Jackson, Artis manufactures arts and crafts glues and adhesive supplies. In addition to its Aleene's Original Tacky Glue division, the firm also produces a monthly magazine, Aleene's Creative Living (circulation 160,000) published by Time Warner's Oxmoor House; films in its Buellton television studios a program aired daily on The Nashville Network; and runs a color printing shop.

But three years ago the firm ran into a series of problems. It lacked sufficient working capital as it expanded. Its Tijuana glue-bottling plant was beset with flooding problems and lost about $500,000 of inventory to thieves over four months.

Its financial books reflected $2.2 million in unsecured debt and another $2.4 million in secured debt. The company filed for Chapter 11 bankruptcy protection on Nov. 17, 1993, in U.S. Bankruptcy Court in Santa Barbara. Under Chapter 11, a company can keep creditors at bay while reorganizing.

Before filing, the company took steps to improve its

profitability and management focus. In late 1993, the company hired the Los Angeles-based corporate revitalization firm of Buccino and Associates to evaluate the business and decide which product lines to cease and which to continue.

It laid-off employees and closed its money-losing wood products line, based in Buellton. Four senior executives took substantial salary cuts, according to court papers.

When Artis Inc. filed for bankruptcy protection, court records indicated at least one healthy sign — the company had a backlog of $1.8 million in orders for its glue products.

Company officials took the bold but risky step of asking larger customers for pre-payment on outstanding orders.

"We were virtually shut down when we filed," Hershman said. "All but one of our top 40 customers pre-paid half their orders; that raised $500,000 in three days — enough to restart the company."

For the next 20 months, the employees committed themselves to saving the company, Hershman said, with salaried people working 16 to 18 hour days.

"Our people saved the company," he said. "It was a real team effort."

Artis closed its Tijuana plant and new contracts with a new partner in Fresno to bottle its glues and

adhesives.

The company reinvented its consumer services department in Buellton, where about 45 employees answer 3,000 to 5,000 phone calls daily from customers placing orders or asking questions about craft products.

"We're handling eight to nine times more calls now than before we filed," Hershman said. "That's a great service to our customers."

Another 40,000 to 60,000 pieces of mail arrive each month at the Buellton plant, where workers open them to answer questions and fill orders for free idea sheets, Jackson said.

Jackson has decided to license her well-known brand name — Aleene's — to two separate companies for paint and glue sticks. Artis is presently evaluating proposed licensing agreements with other companies and categories.

With these steps, the company signed off on its bankruptcy papers last July 14, Hershman said.

All this went unseen by viewers of "Aleene's Creative Living" television show. This April, the program will be expanded from 30 minutes to one hour of original programming every day, Jackson said. That means more filming at the Buellton studio, housed in the former Birkholm's Bakery building.

Aleene with Fred's son Spencer, and great grandchildren from left to right: Kaila, Joshua, Savanah and Austin.

CHAPTER TWELVE

Crafting My Philosophy

When I decided it was time for the kids to take over, I sold my stock in Artis/Aleene, Inc., and turned over management to Tony, as president, Fred, as vice president, Tiffany, as emcee and production director of our television show as well as the editor of our magazine, *Aleene's Creative Living*, and Heidi, as our designer, in addition to her projects for other companies. As I was pondering what to do after the kids took over, many people said, "Why don't you write a book on your life, Aleene?" A few others added, "What's your philosophy of life, anyway?"

Well, I'm not a philosopher, far from it. But through my experiences over the years, as well as through my reading, listening, and learning from other people, I've come to some conclusions about life that I want to share in this chapter.

When I was first thinking about how I would write this book, I decided that the most important thing I wanted to say was that I didn't start with everything handed to me. I had a minimal education, and really wasn't interested in books or learning when I was a kid (although I did become a reader and appreciator of books in later years). Nothing in school prepared me for the directions my life would take, and I had no special training. Certainly I wasn't born with a silver spoon in my mouth. But in spite of everything, I was able to make my way in the world, able to develop myself into a successful businesswoman, and able to help launch, along with a few others, a whole new field which has now grown to a multi-billion-a-year industry.

What did I have going for me that made me different from other women of my era? (It was a time, I have to add, when women were not encouraged to develop their skills and talents outside the home, and yet I was, right from the start.)

Looking back on it, I realize that I had a certain inner drive, a determination to go my own way, regardless of what other people thought or said about me. I remember that when I started the Equine Club during my high school years, and the principal wanted it to be part of the official school functions but I didn't want it to be, I stuck to my guns in the face of authority. And, years later, when the Southern California Hobby Industry Association didn't want to see their way to letting a woman be president, I fought them with everything I had, until they had to agree to let me assume the leadership of the organization to which I'd been elected.

I guess one of the cornerstones of my philosophy, if I have one, would be to "let your light shine." Or as they say in those advertisements for the U.S. Army, "Be All That You Can Be."

Don't be afraid to express yourself. Your thoughts and your ideas for how you want things to be are important. I think a lot of us grow up encircled by limitations, but most of these limitations, in thought and in action, are self-imposed, meaning we put them on ourselves. Yes, that's right, self-imposed. I remember something I read once from Nelson Mandela, though I don't have the exact quote, saying that people think they're afraid of their limitations, but what they're really afraid of is finding out just how magnificent and unlimited they are! I think I first learned about the idea of our unlimited potential from the teachings of the Church of Religious Science, now called Science of Mind.

I guess part of my philosophy has to do with the idea that I believe anything is possible. That's one of the reasons I loved Richard Bach's book, *Illusions*. In it people walk through brick walls and so forth, which I believe is possible. I just think we can't do it yet because we don't know how to think like that. Only a short time ago, it seemed impossible that you could send somebody up to land on the moon. And today it seems impossible that a person can walk through a brick wall, but who's to say that we aren't someday going to learn how to do it?

My husband, Gail, was a great fan of Bach's books, *Jonathan Livingston Seagull, Illusions*, and *A Bridge Across Forever*, due, in good measure, to the author's interest in aviation, and how he used flying to tell stories about expanding our consciousness. And his book *A Bridge Across Forever* is the perfect story, of how a marriage should be. In that story, the husband learns from the wife, and she learns from him, and together they learn about life. After all, marriage is meant to be a shared, learning experience, and Richard Bach captured that beautifully. Too bad it doesn't always work out like that.

Another aspect of my personal philosophy has to do with taking responsibility for ourselves. It's too easy to blame everyone else for your troubles, starting with your parents and going on down the line to your siblings and classmates, to people you encounter in your world. I believe in taking personal responsibility for whatever happens. And I guess I was lucky, because my dad always said I could do what I wanted, as long as I was ready to take full responsibility for it. Naturally, that made me think twice before I went out and did something stupid. But it also gave me a healthy respect for the power of the individual to do something and to take responsibility for it.

One thing curious thing I've found over the years is that there are an awful lot of people who do something and don't want to share it. They are afraid it will be taken from them, that perhaps maybe their ideas would be "stolen." I could never understand that approach. If you keep it to yourself, it's never going to do any good. Pretty soon somebody comes out with a similar idea and beats you to it anyway. Better to develop your idea, program or project, and develop a confidence to bring it to the public, whether it's in your hometown community, the nation, or the world, for that matter. Don't be afraid that someone's going to steal your idea. Don't even think about that. Keep your focus on what it is you're trying to accomplish. Keep looking forward and you'll find yourself headed in the right direction.

Along those lines, (I know I have mentioned this before, but I have to say it again), every problem is really an opportunity in disguise, whether in our personal lives or in our business lives. Let's say you're having a problem with one of your children. Let's say it's already gone to the point where there is no communication, you're not calling them back and they're not calling you back. Both sides are angry about something or other, and they're both stubborn about holding to their respective positions. Now what? Now you've created the opportunity for one or both to realize that they can't hold this position forever. Someone's going to have to give in, let go. And in so doing, one or both now have the opportunity to expand their consciousness by forgiving the other. The parent, the child, or both, now have the opportunity to express compassion for each other and understanding for what the other believes in: Or at least, it allows them their belief or position. I know these challenges aren't easy, but isn't it true that we grow mostly through resolving our conflicts?

Another opportunity of the kind I'm talking about came when Aurora, Inc., bought my company all those years ago. As soon as the ink was dry on the contracts I knew I'd made a mistake letting them take over my "baby." Yet here was a problem, and a big one for me, which had in it the kernels of an opportunity. During the year or so that they were running Aleene's, Inc., I took the opportunity to learn new crafts which had always interested me but which I'd never had the time for. Later, when I had the company back, I was able to turn some of what I learned during that time into new craft products for Artis/Aleene's, Inc. So look for those moments that appear to be problems. They are really opportunities for you to grow and change.

I mentioned that when I was younger, I hardly read much at all; too busy with horses, then later, too busy running my florist shop and subsequent businesses, and raising a family. But eventually, and luckily for me, I started to read more and more. I don't know for sure how I have found the time, but I've been reading quite a bit in the last two decades, especially books about the "human potential movement," as some people have called it; maybe I should just say books about how we grow and expand throughout our lives.

These days, I'm very turned on by writers who are being called "New Age," although many of their teachings and ideas are as old as the hills, if not older! My favorites today include all of Richard Bach's books, and books by people like Louise Hay. Her book, *Heal Yourself*, John Kabat Zinn's book *Wherever You Go, There You Are*, and of course, any books by Deepak Chopra are at the top of my list. I've been a long time fan of Ayn Rand's books, ever since my daughter Candy turned me on to *Atlas Shrugged* and *The Fountainhead*, many years ago. I recall Candy telling me one night on the phone about Ayn Rand's work, that I would enjoy her point of view, and I did. Up until then, I hadn't really had the time or inclination to read much, and when Candy suggested I read Ayn Rand's book *Atlas Shrugged*, boy, was I surprised. It was my philosophy, everything she was writing about was what I believed. In fact, later I made a special trip to New York and actually heard Ayn Rand speak. In person and in her many novels and essays, was that she fully believed in the power of the individual above all else, and so do I.

I don't know whether we learn from books, or whether they just reinforce what we already believe and agree upon. In many cases, I already had thoughts similar to what the writer was suggesting, so maybe their words just reinforced what I already knew to be true for me. In a way, that's one of the great things about books. Aside from giving

I had a wonderful opportunity to meet Deepak Chopra at a television appearance at the "Home Show" on ABC. It was a thrill, as he is one of my very favorite authors.

us new ideas to think about, they can also help confirm things we've previously believed in. Maybe we thought we were the only ones who believed it, but reading someone else's vision of the same idea confirms your own beliefs in a new way. Up until then, I think the only things I had read had come from the Church of Religious Science literature. I taught Sunday School there, and the kids even went to a Church of Religious Science type of school. I was active in supporting the church and everything, but I had a disagreement with the minister, a woman. Don't get me wrong, she was a wonderful woman. To me, she wasn't even in this world--she was out of this world. By her study, and self-study, she had aready graduated out of this world. In short, a very unusual person. But, when she said to me, that everything works on faith, I just couldn't be convinced about it. Then, somebody came to a meeting of the board of the Hobby Association at my home and deliberately left a book by Thomas Paine, *The Age of Reason*. I started reading it and it made me wonder. Paine shows the the inconsistencies in the *Bible*, and points out why being an atheist or agnostic might make some sense. Then I thought I was an agnostic, which Webster defines as, "a person who believes that the human mind cannot know whether there is a God or an ultimate cause or anything beyond material phenomena," because I believed in nature. I believe in the wind, even if I can't see it, I can still feel it. I guess my problem was that churches were built by people, and I had no faith in people. I had faith in a Great Spirit, as the American Indians call it, and I knew there was a spirit, but I didn't have faith that the minister necessarily had more of an access to it than I did or you do.

That was my changeover at the time I first read Ayn Rand's *Atlas Shrugged*. Of course, she was an atheist, but still I liked what she had to say about the power of the individual, and the need for each of us to know our own power. But power is not enough-- you have to have compassion, too. So I started expanding the kind of books I read, broadening my own understanding through the works and words of others. So all of these books led me up to my philosophy. Of course, you take the parts you like, and ignore what you don't like. I don't want to be a person who reads a book and believes everything. I want to take what I believe in from a book and try to use it in my life where I can.

Speaking of religion, I guess you know by now that I'm not a big believer in organized religion. I feel that I'm a spiritual person, but organized religion has never really appealed to me. I suppose there are people for whom it works, and since I believe you need to go with what works, I'm not putting it down. But for me, the important thing is that I find my own connection with spirit, that's what works best for me. Maybe it's because of something that happened to me in a church many years ago. I was delivering flowers before a wedding, and the minister came on to me in a sexual way. First of all, I was barely twenty-one years old, and I couldn't believe it was happening. That he was a man of the cloth made it even stranger, I guess, and it scared the hell out of me. My first thought was, wait a minute-- this guy is the spiritual leader of a bunch of people who think he's a good man. If I hadn't been fast on my feet, what would have happened? The event was extremely disorienting to me because up until then, in my innocence, I believed that members of the clergy had to be good people. Oh, we had some scandalous "radio preachers," back in those days, but by and large, you didn't see or hear about any of the horrible scandals you hear about today.

The bottom line, of course, is that my beliefs about God or the Great Spirit, really matter only to me. I've never tried to foist my belief system on anyone else, and I'm sure, you're like me, in that we don't feel comfortable when someone's trying to convince us that their way of thinking is right. I heard somewhere that "there are many paths to God, but they all lead to the same place," and that makes sense to me. That's what our country was founded on, don't forget. And in my opinion, that freedom to worship how we choose, to belive in what we wish to believe in, is what has made America great.

I keep hearing a lot on the news about "giving people self-esteem," but you can't give anybody self-esteem, they have to earn it. And, in my opinion, people don't seem to understand that concept of earning anymore.

How do you earn your self-esteem? There are a million different ways, in big things and little things. Take the simple idea of doing a job well, whatever that job is. If you're a waitress, find your self-esteem in knowing that you do a really good job of serving people; you're a mom and you took the time to create a lovely little birthday party for one of your kids, whether the kid appreciated it or not, you know you did it really well and did everything you were supposed to do so that everybody enjoyed themselves. In everything we do, there is the opportunity to gain some self-respect, some self-esteem, provided that we approach our tasks with the idea that "I'm going to do this to the best of my ability." I know this is simplistic, but give it a try. I think you'll be surprised at the results.

Thinking about self-esteem leads me back to the period of the Great Depression of the 30s, when I lived at 118 E. Broadway in San Gabriel. There were train tracks right behind us, like the main line for the Santa Fe Railroad, and there were tramps who would get off right behind our house. We always fed them when they knocked on our door. And we always gave them some work to do in exchange. In those days what we now call "homeless" people wanted to work. They never just asked for handouts. there were poor people, but they didn't lose their self-esteem. Even though they didn't have money, and times were horrible economically, they kept their self-esteem by trading work for what they got from you. We were always feeding someone when we lived there. And you were never afraid of them, there was never any violence. I don't remember any violence when I was young. I don't understand how people have been conditioned to the violence now. I pray that it will swing back the other way. I know it will, I just wonder when.

I'm glad the forces that be are realizing finally that self-esteem is very important when we're children, when we're in the process of growing up. Because once you develop it, your self-esteem in turn gives you additional energy and gumption to move through each phase of your life. And that's why I think arts and crafts are so great, really, for developing values and a sense of self-worth. Because when a child does something, creates something, they gain a little more self-esteem then they had before. Then they know they can go on and do another project, perhaps an even more challenging one the next time.

Of course, I have a bone to pick with the way children are being taught, and have been taught, ever since I was young. In kindergarten, for instance, in painting or drawing, children are told to draw a tree. But they're not told how. So they all draw a tree as they saw it in their mind. But in most cases, the teacher has neglected to say, "Let's go out and look at a tree. See how the sun hits it? On this side it's light, on this side it's dark?" Not knowing the children are not successful, and they know it. They might look at that drawing and feel it wasn't very good. That in turn leads them to think that maybe they aren't very good. Until at about 25 years old or so, I'd get them in my arts and crafts classes at a point when they felt that they could never do anything good with their talents. But, as I realized in my teaching days, it was simply because they had never been taught basics. So teaching is very, very important, how we teach and how we learn.

That's why I loved the recent movie, *Mr. Holland's Opus*, with Richard Dreyfuss. It's about a teacher and the great way he taught. If all teachers taught like that, every child would thoroughly like school. though I had a few good teachers, by and large I had some pretty lousy ones. I failed English one term simply because I just couldn't stand the teacher. I got no help, no understanding, and so I just failed. With education, you can lead a horse to water but you can't make it drink. From the time of kindergarten, you have to help children see that school is a precious gift to them. You're not really going to help them unless they come to ask for help. To tell them to sit there and do their homework, for an hour or two hours or whatever, never works. By the time kids get to that age, they're gonna fight you every inch of the way. If you're always available to help them, that's great. I didn't have time to sit there and be a policeman over my children. I think my parents were probably the same way. I always felt that education was up to me. However much I learned was how much I was going to get in life, how much money I was going to make and how I was going to get to do the things I wanted to.

I didn't think when I was growing up that it was important for me to try to go to college. If I'd been planning to be a doctor or something, then obviously I would have gone. But I couldn't see myself going to college just for fun, which was the reason most gals, like my sisters-in-law, went. They went for fun, and, of course, to find a husband. But I wanted to get out and start working, doing something.

Speaking of working, I think we're all basically a little lazy. Perhaps it's biological, but I know that there are lots of times when I'm real tired, but if I force myself to get up and get going, I'm surprised that I quickly get over being lazy and can accomplish so much. Of course, I make lots of lists. I have a list every day of what I'm going to accomplish. I don't necessarily accomplish even a fraction of it, but then it goes to the next day list. At night, I usually make a new list for the next day. By making a list, you see what's important. My father was always real cute about that. When he came to work with me and was running the company, he had In and Out baskets. But once it got to be two weeks old he just threw out the correspondence. Even though he had a secretary, his attitude was that if it wasn't worth answering right away, it wasn't worth it. I'm sure you'll agree that's a little bit of an extreme filing system, but it worked for him.

I mentioned earlier in this book that I know I was very lucky that my family didn't force "girl" things on me at all. when I was little, I had a doll or two, and a tea set, that type of thing. But my parents also involved me in building projects, showing me at a very early age how to hammer, how to saw, and how to put things together. Any time my dad was building, I joined in and helped. And my grandfather, with whom I was so close, always was showing me things about his carpentry projects.

Today, probably as a result, all my daughters are very handy, every one of them. Candy's husband can't repair anything. She had enough of that and put herself in charge of repairs in their house. Tiffany is also very independent and able to fix anything. Although Heidi's current husband, Butch, is extremely handy, there were times that she was a single mom and had to fix things herself. My boys, Fred and Tony, are of course, super handy.

For a long while now, I've been collecting information that I might use for nation-wide seminars I'd like to organize, about empowering women. And I'd like your help, too, if you think this would be worthwhile to pursue.

I think that even with the growing interest (thank God!) in women's issues, and all the many seminars I've seen advertised in the last twenty years since the women's movement really began to flower, there aren't too many of them that focus on the practical, down-to-earth issues that are of value to the female gender: If you think that this would be of interest, please write me (in care of this publisher) and let me know your ideas for a seminar on Empowering Women. What would you like to see in such a program? Please write me in care of this publisher, and I will gladly try and incorporate your ideas into what I'm developing.

One of the first things that would be presented in these seminars would be to teach women practical information, like setting up records for their personal and business lives. Basic things that go along with starting a small business, like how you set up files, mail, telephones, office equipment, legal matters and how to get bank loans, licenses, permits and so forth would certainly be included.

From my experience, being in business for yourself is good. Many women work at 9-to-5 jobs, that makes it difficult to even consider starting something of their own. And, if you're a mother, you've got to work twice as hard. But if you have an idea, or a dream of getting into your own business, our Empowering Women program would provide direction and encouragement in making your dream a reality.

Back in the earliest days of my company, everyone in my family always had more than one job. Things were so tight back then that it took at least two jobs to be able to support a household. We were always working on something else, too, dreaming and striving for something different. As I've said earlier, you can't just say that you have a good idea and decide to go into business. You've got to work on it over time, just like my daughter Heidi is doing right now. She's been so busy doing 20 new ideas a month for Oxmoor House. She wrote a book called *Craft Quickies*, and all this time she's been putting together a children's book called *Where Do Angels Buy Their Clothes?* She had to do these other things in order to have enough money to develop her own business, to publish her own books, which isn't easy and isn't cheap. I admire her spirit and determination, and it's the very kind of thing I'd like to be able to encourage and present to women of all ages and all walks of life through Empowering Women Seminars.

I think a lot of women out there are nurturing dreams and aspirations of being in business for themselves. They've just never had someone to give them the information, direction and confidence in order for them to achieve that goal; and the inspiration, too. But if there's any possible way that on Saturdays or Sundays, for example, you can set aside some time to do what you want to do, then go for it. Sure, it might take two years or five years to grow to the point where you can go into it full-time, but you'll be quietly building toward the time when you can do your own business in your own way.

Part of the problem, of course, has been that in the past, women have been treated differently than men. Throughout history, women were brought up to believe that their purpose on Earth was to be a mother, plain and simple. It's only in the 20th century that major strides have been made for women's equality. Today, young women are learning that they have creative ideas just as wonderful as the men have (and often better), and that they have skills and talents that should be compensated equally with men. But in spite of the gains made for women, even nowadays you don't see a lot of women in very high places in business. The "glass ceiling" is still a reality in most of corporate America, let alone the rest of the world.

For some reason, probably my childhood upbringing, believing that I was as good as any man in business, just happened to be normal for me. When I first got into business, running my own little florist shop, I didn't know I was doing anything different. Although at that time, a woman owning a business was still pretty unique. But I just did it, and I guess I was aggressive with it. Curiously enough, the time that I had to fight for a woman to be president of the Southern California Hobby Industry Association, was the only time I can remember actually fighting for something that I believed was my right, and that was being denied because I wasn't a man. Outside of that, I had no problems at all that I can remember. I guess I never considered myself just a woman. I considered myself a businessperson. I didn't question it, so the people I came into contact with didn't either.

One of my pet peeves is that women are never taught to bank. When I started my florist shop, I thought I didn't need any money. But somebody told me to go to the bank and borrow anyway; borrow $100, pay it off in six months, I was told. Keep that hundred, and pay it off, plus the interest. Six months later, borrow again, to show that you're responsible. This will enable you to borrow more money, especially once your business is off and running, and in the process you've gotten yourself a good reputation. In my family, I always did all the check writing, and so I had a handle on where we were, financially speaking. Learn the ins and outs about your banking system, as it affects you; the hidden charges, and ways to save so that your money can earn interest and work for you.

I also find that many women have no idea about insurance, or other practical aspects of personal and business life. Instead of teaching these practical things to young girls, our society has focused, in the past, on home economics, things like learning to cook.

Well, as they say, enough about me. In the next chapter, my five children, Candy, Fred, Heidi, Tiffany and Tony, share their thoughts with you, about me, about themselves, and growing up with Artis/Aleene's, Inc. I've enjoyed telling you my story, and I hope that some of my experiences and thoughts were entertaining, at the least, and educational, at the most.

Stay tuned for the sequel. As George Burns said at the gala celebration of his ninetieth birthday, "It's been a great life, and now I'm looking forward to the second half."

Aleene

--Aleene

nk You for your support and encouragement. Your friendship, both on a personal and professional
vel has made the difference. It is with renewed strength, we enter this new season. The staff and
management of Aleene's is committed to serving you better than ever. The difficulties that we've
experienced last year are behind us and we have the motivation, financial strength and
production capacity to deliver Aleene's Tacky Glue and the other Aleene's fine craft
products throughout the season and beyond.

e have consolidated the Aleene's line to the most popular products and sizes to better serve you.
The "Tacky Glue Team" has been working together to increase production to maintain the
stock necessary to fulfill your needs through the coming months. If you have
requirements regarding catalog, ad items or special request, please contact
the sales team for help with these special circumstances.

Thank You.

At this point I want to give my personal thanks to all of the dedicated
associates for their help during the bankruptcy.

This was a recent picture (Christmas 1995) of the kids that are currently involved in the business, from left to right. Candy (not pictured) has been involved in other projects with me, Heidi and Tiffany. She also appears periodically on our "Aleene's Creative Living" Television Show, as an herbalist. The next chapter was designed to have each one of the kids share their experiences growing up with the "Queen of Crafts."

CHAPTER THIRTEEN

A Few Words from the Kids

I decided I wanted my kids to give some of their thoughts on their lives growing up with me in this book, but first I'll introduce them to you:

Candy Liccione, Born January 6, 1947

Candy was one of the most beautiful babies I'd ever seen. She had a beautiful face and she laughed a lot. I remember that she didn't like school, though she loved reading and loved books. In that regard, she was very much like her father. She wasn't outgoing, really, and I know that at first she had a rough time in school. It wasn't that she wasn't smart, because she was, but she just wasn't the type that liked being in school. I kept pushing her into joining this and that, and doing this and that, but what she really liked to do was to sit and read. Candy was reading when she was 5 years old. She read everything in the children's library, and I had to take her to the adult library and get her a card. That's all she really wanted to do. But I pushed her to go to dances and do a lot of things she didn't want to do.

As a result of my mistake of pushing her to be

like me, she had to leave home to get away from me. In high school, Candy had an advisor who recommended she go to secretarial school. I remember that there were two good ones that had been suggested to her, one in San Diego, not too far from where we were, and one in Boston, way over on the other side of the continent. They said that Katherine Gibbs' School in Boston was the very best secretarial school in the country, so we flew back to Boston so she could visit and see if she wanted to enroll. She decided she did. Then we went to New York, where the World's Fair was on. I taped a television show with Shari Lewis, the gal who had the puppets. Then we came home, and Candy flew back later to start school.

Starting with day one, Candy phoned every night wanting to come home. Each night I kept saying, "stay there," hoping it would work for her. She finally stayed for the two years, and it was there she met Peter, who became her first husband. Unfortunately, he became a hippie and got into drugs, and it took quite some time for her to make up her mind to leave him and that situation.

Because she had such good training and secretarial background, she took a job, again away from me, in S--- Francisco. That was where she met Ed, her husban --- --m she's married to now. Ed and she are very goc --- --ch other, and I know Candy really grew in her marriage to Ed. She's the mother of my grandson Shaun, now twenty-six. And Candy is also a wonderful hostess, who does really beautiful interior decorating. For a time, she worked for somebody in a wicker shop, and that was what gave her the nerve to start one of her own. Candy finally has realized her own wonderful abilities, so it's been fun to see her growing.

Today, Candy and I are in touch by phone almost every day. I probably will never be as close with my kids as are some mothers who were really full-time mothers are. As I've said in the book, our housekeeper, Audrey, was in some ways more of a mother to my kids than I was. She was there day in and day out, while I was putting in hours and hours in the business. Audrey was there for the kids full-time, and even when I was home, my mind was often times still on my business. Even when we took trips, they generally consisted of some sales job or other. If the kids fell and scraped themselves, Audrey was the one who was there to pick them up and to nurse their cuts.

Today Candy and I have tremendous respect for each other and I'm delighted at whom she's become. I like to think of Candy as the spiritual leader in our family. She's been the one who would call me or the other kids to talk about new books she'd read, new ways of thinking about things, like spiritual growth, human potential, and stuff like that. And whenever she makes a suggestion to me, I go right out and get the book, or listen to the tape. And usually her instincts and intuition are right on the mark!

From the desk of Candy.

Looking back, it seems like we were always working when we were kids. Mom's motto was always "work is play," so we didn't need to play. We worked everywhere, in the wholesale department at Aleene's, mail order, retail, gift shop, you name it. We counted stamens and did whatever work there was to do. It also depended on how old you were. When we were real little some tasks were beyond our capabilities, but we did a lot of mailings and other things, too.

I remember that Aleene took us with her a lot. There were also times when we sat in the car when she used to go visit the dealers or crafts shops. She also took us on many of her early television tapings. I remember running around the TV stations, playing, (and how the people at the studios really loved that).

This was Candy around age 6, on her way to school.

As kids, we grew up in Mom's business. We took every class that was given, like wood fibre flowers or whatever the flower of the week was. When she had the retail store in Temple City I remember that we took every single class.

Today I'm married to a wonderful man, Ed Liccone, and I have one child, a son, named Shaun. He's twenty-six and lives in Baltimore. I've opened my own business in Royersford, Pennsylvania, called The Herbal Sanctuary. My husband Ed and I moved here about a year-and-a-half ago because I wanted more land to grow herbs, and wanted a place with several buildings where I could develop my work. We have seven acres, and I have a separate 30' x 30' building, which is the Herbal Sanctuary.

Our house has a Frank Lloyd Wright-inspired design. You could call it American contemporary. It's on seven acres, partly woods and partly yard. With: A nature trail that goes through habitats, which is probably about two acres. And a trail that goes through the woods, and a creek. Nearby is a big pond. There's a children's playground and playhouse, a little picnic pavilion, and a gazebo, and a building with the herb shop in it, where the classes are being held. People who've heard about the Herbal Sanctuary through *Creative Living Magazine* are calling and wanting to come by. One group from Texas wants to come on a retreat. So, I thought maybe it would be a retreat place. But then when I got here I wasn't sure how that would work, or if it would work. As a family living here, I didn't think that would really be comfortable for my husband.

Years ago, I worked in a wicker store and learned a great deal about flower arranging. An acquaintance of mine had started the store and I just went in and volunteered to help her as an apprentice. I think I worked for her a good year without pay. But I learned everything. I stayed with her for about two years and ended up managing the store. Then I opened my own gift shop, that I had for 7 years. While I learned most of my business practices like how to buy and how to run a business, from my friend, I know I learned how to work from Mom.

When we were kids, Mom made us buy a lot of our clothes. She always felt we needed to learn the value of money; so we worked and worked and worked. I can remember working the mail order for Grandma, and getting 25¢ a day. As I recall, Mom didn't pay us, but Grandma did.

I have wonderful memories of my grandparents, Aleene's mother and father. They were filled with true, unconditional love. I always felt that they loved us just as we were. Without them, we probably would have been really messed up, but somehow their love balanced everything out. They knew their daughter quite well. They knew she was a really tough person back then, so Grandpa and Grandma were always there. They did a lot of baby-sitting with us kids. I remember that they used to pay us $2.00 to go to their house and spend the night. And we had their undivided attention when we were at their house. Grandpa Jackson would appear very gruff on occasion, and I remember saying to Grandma Jackson, "Is he really mad, or is he kidding?" But while he had a gruff personality sometimes, he truly loved every one of us. My father's parents, on the other hand, were very harsh disciplinarians, and not at all affectionate.

As a teenager, like Fred, Heidi and Tiffany, I went to Arcadia High School, as did Heidi and Fred, and Tiffany. We were like most families, in that you're close with one or two of your siblings, and maybe not so close with others. I was close with Fred when we were growing up, but I hated Heidi. When I left home to go back east to college, Tiffany was about 8 or 9, so I never really got to know her until much later, when she divorced her husband and came to stay with me. She spent the summer with us and I really got to know her better. It's funny, but Heidi and I didn't really develop a good relationship until we both had our own stores. I used to go to California to the gift show with her, and we've become really close in the last ten years. Since I was the only one of the five children who'd left California, I had more difficulties maintaining a relationship with everybody.

In a funny way, leaving home ultimately wasn't

really my decision. A woman I worked for at the high school suggested it and my boyfriend at the time encouraged me, so it was kind of decided that I was going away. I went along with it because, at the time, everybody was going somewhere, off to college or to jobs. And I had nothing specific I wanted to do, nothing I wanted to be. A woman at my high school pushed me to go to Katherine Gibbs Secretarial School in Boston, a far cry from Southern California.

It's odd, looking back on it, but I really didn't want to go. But when Mom made a fuss saying she didn't want me to go, then I suddenly wanted to. In the long run, for me, it was the best thing I ever did. I didn't do well there. The first two or three weeks I was so homesick, I thought I was going to die. I really wanted to get away, but when I actually got to the East Coast, the reality of being away from my home and family was terrible, and I begged to come home. Mom would have let me come home, but the school wouldn't. She said, "Put her on a plane and send her home."

The school officials at Katherine Gibbs brought me into the office and asked me if I really wanted to throw in the towel after only being there a week or two? "Absolutely!" I said. The lady in the office said she'd make a deal with me, "Stay two more weeks. If you still want to go home after two weeks, we'll let you go home." Of course, in two weeks I had acclimated enough to stay a little longer, and so I ended up completing the whole one-year course.

Then I met my first husband, so I didn't go home that summer. I got out of school in June, 1965, and by August I'd married Peter Dodge, my first husband, who was from Massachusetts. We were married in California, but within a few months, Peter was in a bad motorcycle accident and was in the hospital for about eight months. Mom didn't like him from the start. Not only was he a troublemaker, but he was a beatnik before there were beatniks, way before there were hippies. Peter was exactly the opposite of Mom-- as conservative as she was, he was that far left, politically. In a way, Peter was providing me with a viewpoint that was directly opposite from everything Mom had raised me to believe. It was interesting to me because I had never realized that she had only shown me her side of the world, and that there was a whole different world out there. I didn't necessarily agree with him any more than I agreed with Mom, but leaving home was great because I got to experience a whole world other than the one I'd grown up with.

After Peter got out of the hospital in California, he was still in a partial cast. But we drove back to Boston because we were having so much trouble with Mom. We stayed there for about eight months or so, but then things got bad and he told me to leave. I became ill, and Peter sent me home to California. At the time Mom and Gail were married and living on Bidwell Avenue. That summer Gail's son, David, was there. So, I went back to work for Mom because I got stuck with all of Peter's bills. But I only stayed a short time because it was so restrictive. I'd been married and living on my own, and now back at Mom's house, she wanted me to go to bed at 9 o'clock! So I finally left and moved to San Francisco where I got a job with a mortgage company. Mom swore she'd never speak to me again, but she did.

It was in San Francisco that I met Ed Liccione, who would become my husband. Ed was in the US Army in Alaska, and there he'd been friends with my

This was Candy's wedding to Peter Dodge.

ex-husband's best friend. They had a furlough in San Francisco, and the guy with them said he knew somebody who lived in San Francisco, me. So, Ed literally showed up at my front door with my first husband's best friend. That was 1968. Well, Peter and I weren't divorced yet. I kept thinking maybe we could get back together. We were actually married three years, but we only lived together about a year-and-a-half. Mom wanted me to get a divorce, and was really pushing, but I didn't do it. I started the divorce before I met Ed, but we had to wait until my divorce was final. Ed and I got married in November of 1968.

After I got out of the gift business, I spent about a year taking classes. I was interested in metaphysics then, so I explored past-life regression and took classes in parapsychology. I became interested when I had the store, but I didn't have the time. When I suddenly had the time, I did everything I could to learn about spiritual fulfillment. Then I ended up, at some point, in California, meeting with a psychic named Stephanie Brown, down in Manhattan Beach. I told her I didn't know what I want to do with my life. I'd just gotten rid of my business and taken all these classes, and was interested in metaphysics, but I really didn't know what I wanted to do. Stephanie asked if I'd ever thought about being an herbalist, and I said that I hadn't. She told me to think about it, because it might be something I'd really like. I said, sure, fine, goodbye. But, she had planted a seed. I didn't do anything about it at first. Then I ran across some ads and thought, maybe...

This was Candy's second marriage, to Edward Liccione. At our Church, Santa Anita Church of Religious Science.

I'd always had a green thumb and like mom, I always liked plants. Of course, when we were kids, Mom made gardening torture because that was yard work at home. It wasn't something pleasant and fun. It was picking leaves out of the mulch. Every Saturday morning we did yard work before we could do anything else. But I've always loved plants, and I'm sure that love led to my creating my current project, the Herbal Sanctuary.

Basically, it's more a place where people can come, a sanctuary, than a business or store. I have display gardens, usually with themes such as a medicinal tea gardens. There's an edible plant garden, with different herbs that fit into each theme. People come and visit the gardens, to have herbal lunches. We have tea in the gardens, and a number of classes about herbs and how

Candy, Ed and Shaun.
Shaun is now married this year (1996).

they affect us.

I'm trying to work more on the emotional body than the physical body. And I try to teach people that it all ties together. So that what's going on in their emotional life, is what's going on with their health. Herbs are one of the ways to get people to open up, to get them thinking about their lives and the things that affect them.

To me, herbs are very spiritual. They are a way of getting us into the essence of the plant. What they can do medically, is not as significant as what they can do spiritually. A lot of it is flower lore, but I really go deeper than that. I've done a lot of research and come up with more metaphysics, and less flower lore. A lot of it is more for ceremonial purposes.

If you've read this book this far, you know that as Aleene's children we were raised with a very metaphysical overview. I remember I disagreed with her when I was young. Even back then she said that cancer and other diseases were caused by negative thoughts. Now I realize that she was right about that. I'm very pleased now with the way I was raised, as far as philosophy or metaphysics is concerned. It was very confusing when I was a child. I always felt different, and I had ideas and thoughts that just didn't go along with what other people were saying. Now it all makes sense.

At this point in my life, I know I've absorbed wonderful things from Mom. When I was a child it was extremely difficult being her eldest daughter. I think she even said in an earlier chapter that she tried to force me, (she tried to force all of us) to be like her. We always felt that she never treated us as separate personalities. Being the oldest, I spent my whole childhood trying to keep peace in the family, trying to keep everybody from upsetting her. A lot of people I know have come to terms with their parents, but they really haven't forgiven them. Once I understood how it worked, that forgiveness in everything was the key, I realized that the lessons I had learned were excellent. They made me the person that I am. I feel that as children, we all had self-confidence problems. For many years, I felt like I was the child of a celebrity, and that I could never quite measure up to her. Then, too, you sometimes get the feeling that people were using you to get to your mother. It's like you are nobody, but you're so-and-so's daughter. A lot of people wanted to meet Aleene, to get her autograph, that kind of thing. Nowadays, however, I'm glad that Mom and I have gotten closer. We have a really good relationship now. But it took a lot of hard work on both our parts.

Because of Mom, we all developed an excellent work ethic. We learned how to work because of her, and we learned the value of money.

For a long time when I first lived back in Pennsylvania, I didn't talk to mom. I couldn't deal with her. At about age thirty-five, though, I realized that I didn't want her to die without me making my peace with her. I realized that I had to take the initiative and forgive her, and forgive myself. And the more I got into metaphysics, the more I began to believe that, from spirit, I'd chosen her to be my mother. Once I realized that, it suddenly all made sense! I needed those lessons, and she was the perfect teacher.

Fred with daughters, Emma and Rebecca, and son Spencer at Christmas 1995.

Fred with son Spencer at Christmas 1995.

Fred Hershman,
Born July 18, 1948.

Next came Fred, who was a lot like Woody, his father. Fred was always a very private person, but a very determined person. I remember that as a child in school, he wore a hat, even though it was against the rules. Fred refused to take it off, and there was nothing they could do. He had a mind of his own. He was very athletic, and even rode to school for a time on a unicycle. He learned to play the guitar, but he wouldn't play for anybody but himself. He was very talented. Anything he did, he did well.

When he went into the Coast Guard, I thought maybe he was going to have trouble because there would be authority figures to deal with. But, when it came time for us to go to his graduation in Oakland, he was the top of his class. I almost fell off the bench; to think Fred was the one that got the Coast Guard top award in his class. Fred always loved to sail and ski, but he was a fairly private person. When our divorce came up, I think Fred was about 17 and he was already out of school. I felt he would be much happier with his father than with me. I never knew whether he was unhappy with me or not, but, I didn't keep him at home. I sent him to live with his father because I really felt Fred had so much more in common with his dad.

Over the years, he came to work for me off and on. He was always a very, very good worker. When we had mailings to do, he was ten times as fast as any of us. He was the only one who set the pace for stuffing envelopes Everything he did, he did quickly and well. Everybody at Artis/Aleene's, Inc., loves Fred.

Fred U.S. Coast Guard 1968.

This was Fred with his Welsh pony "Geronimo" in 1957.

From the desk of Fred.

I was in the Coast Guard for four years on active duty, and two years in the reserve. I was stationed out of San Francisco in 1968. Out of four years, we were in San Francisco for 75 days. We had ocean stations called November and Victor. November is halfway between Hawaii and San Francisco. Ocean station Victor is halfway between Hawaii and Japan. We were at the stations for 30 or 60 day shifts. During that time, I went to Hawaii 19 times, to Alaska twice, and off the coast of Vietnam for a year-and-a-half.

We also went to Singapore, Bangkok, Hong Kong, Borneo, Calcutta and Rangoon. I think we traveled about 100,000 miles in four years.

This was Fred at 16 years old at Lake Arrowhead. This was the second sail boat that we had, and Fred became quite a sailor.

I had my 21st birthday out at one of the ocean stations, an unforgettable birthday because Aleene sent me a "birthday party in a box." I'll always remember it, because the ship that came to relieve us the day before my birthday brought with it Aleene's gift.

Suddenly they were unloading a large box, about the size of a six-foot trunk, with my name on it. Inside, there were cake pans, cake mix, frosting, tablecloths, presents, balloons and a variety of other surprises. She had mailed it so that the timing was perfect. All the guys and I had a great big party, with an instant cake and everything. Then, we had lots of helium, so we filled all the balloons, strapped everything into a big ball and launched it.

I remember starting to work with the family business at around ten years old. We first worked with my grandmother, who handled the mail order division. My dad was in charge of the printing. He photographed things and then printed them.

Aleene taught us all to be self-sufficient, and how to work. She always bought us enough stuff to go to school with, but as we got older and wanted bigger things, like water-skis or boats, we bought them ourselves. I bought a 14-foot sailboat that Aleene co-signed for me. I paid $45.92 a month for a year, and I remember it vividly. Of course, her philosophy was that as kids, we took better care of things if we paid for them ourselves; same went for washing and drying our own clothes. As soon as we could, we washed our own clothes. It's kind of the way our whole lives have been.

Aleene was doing a lot of TV shows in L.A., and everywhere she went, she took us. If we drove to San Francisco we'd stop at every hobby or model shop along the way. We'd sit in the car while she went in and did her sales thing. We stopped in San Luis Obispo, Fresno, Porterville, and up and down the California coast. When we went to Hawaii we stopped at the craft stores, and in New York, the same thing. Sometimes it seemed like our whole life was going from one craft store to another.

I remember that Aleene was in charge of the Hobby Building out at the county fair for a couple of years. I remember it because at the time, I must have been 10 or 11 years old, she coerced all the manufacturers of model airplanes, the gas-driven kind, to donate the models to the show. They made this mockup of an airport, maybe 80 or 100 feet long. They had all donated the stuff and when the show closed, they didn't want it back. So Aleene said, "If you want to put 'em in a box, you can have 'em all." There were 80 or 90 of them, and it took us maybe eight years to destroy them systematically, one by one. We'd fly 'em until they were just no good anymore. It was like "kid heaven" for me.

We were also the beneficiaries of items and products that were demonstrated on Aleene's TV shows. Everytime she had somebody on the show, they'd give her something they had demonstrated. One day the guest was a guy who made go-carts, but the one demonstrated didn't have a motor. So the next week she had to have a guy from the engine company on the show, and we'd get a motor. I remember we got a mini-bike the same way. First we got the frame, then we got a motor. We always had boxes of crafts and things that we never used. Every closet had stuff in it.

I remember when Aleene and Woody bought the Flexible bus, which was the size of a big Greyhound. It was painted red, white and blue. We used it to campaign for Aleene's good friend John Rousselot in his run for Congress, stopping at shopping centers and super-markets to pass out balloons and campaign literature. Then later, after he was elected, we decided to take the bus on a cross-country trip to New York and Washington, D.C. We were going to visit the Rousselots, who were now living in Washington, and they were going to show us around the capital, but halfway across the country, we broke down in Tulsa, Oklahoma. The whole family had to get on a Continental Trailways bus the rest of the way. That was a real experience, from Oklahoma to Washington, D.C. by bus. We stayed with the Rousselots and we actually drove his car with his Congressional plates on it, around Washington, so we could park anywhere we wanted to. It was like we had the run of the capital.

From there, Aleene and Woody took us on to New York City. Because our Flexibus had broken down in Tulsa, we didn't bring any suitcases with us, just bedrolls with all our immediate needs wrapped up in them. I remember that we checked into the prestigious Waldorf-Astoria Hotel with those bedrolls. We raised more than a few eyebrows in the lobby of that place. But for us it was just part of normal, everyday living.

As we got older we did everything in the busi-ness, from loading trucks to working in the art depart-ment. I also worked a lot in the print shop. Then I left Aleene's and got a job at a hamburger stand for a cou-ple of years. It was in Arcadia, a place called Kenny's Drive-In. It was a one-of-a-kind thing, not a chain, dur-ing the old 19¢ hamburger days. There were about three hundred things on the menu: every kind of sand-wich, hamburgers, pastrami, cheese dips, things like that. Then my mother and father got divorced around that time. I moved in with my father, and we lived in an apartment just a couple blocks from the factory.

My dad bought a 25-foot boat, we used to stay on it during weekends down in Newport Beach. And then he thought it would be fun to live on one. So he bought a bigger boat and I went to live with him on it.

I remember that my father came and told me he and Aleene were splitting up. He said, "If you want to, you can come and live with me." That was the end of the session. It wasn't a very big deal. I don't really sweat that kind of thing. To me, it was a very minor detail in my life. My life didn't change that much either, because they still worked together. Nobody was yelling at each other. Nobody was angry.

For a time, I worked with my dad after he left the business. A couple of years later I went back to work for Aleene's. At the time, her company was mainly doing custom packaging. I remember that there were candle molds, shrink-wrapping books for the Huntington Library and packaging for a variety of things. Those were really lean times. We had to think about whether we were going to buy a screwdriver or not. It was really hard work, too. At the time, I didn't really have anything to do with the management of the company. I just worked there, and didn't know it was growing into the big business it would become.

When Aleene and Gail came up with Shrink-Art, she and I traveled all over the country promoting it. Aleene has always had a knack for getting free time on TV. Since she started in TV, when it was really young, she has had lots of contacts. And she's really natural on TV. She went through the book, published every year of all the local TV shows she knew, who the host was, where it was, and the size of the audience. She called and booked guest appearances on one TV show after another. It was like a smaller version of the Craft Caravan, where she set up everything in advance from one city to the next.

Oddly enough, we had the concept, but we hadn't actually identified the source for the finished Shrink Art product yet. I recall that Aleene and I went to Arizona first. We bought a van in Los Angeles right in the middle of the gas crisis. The van had a 50-gallon gas tank on it, a brand new Ford van. We loaded everything into cartons that were 1'x2'x3'. Everything was mounted on the panels that fit in the cartons. There were 33 of these cartons in the van. Aleene had her typewriter-- she always typed as we drove across country. We went to Arizona and did a TV show there.

We'd rented a meeting room at the Holiday Inn, but really had no idea if anybody would show up. But the first show was a mob scene. Everybody came. We'd fold this thing up, put it in the van, and drive at night to the next place to do a TV show. In the parking lots, I would sit in the back of the van and sell Aleene's How-To books to help pay our expenses. We did that for about six months.

During the trip, Aleene would fly home periodically, while I stayed on the road with the van. She would fly home, do some business, and see Gail and the family, while I'd be driving on to the next city. And I'd be there at the airport to pick her up when she flew in from California. With Shrink-Art, we were taking orders across the country and sending them back. By that time, Gail and the team at the plant had identified the right source for the product and were already packaging it. Even when we got back, we were packaging it night and day and on weekends. As quick as we could

Fred was married to Constance Milligan, in Scottland in 1977.

package it, we shipped it.

Just about the time that we had ridden that wave, Aleene decided she wanted to move to Solvang. We flew up there and looked at all kinds of property. Then Aleene and Gail found the property they wanted and bought it. They moved up to Buellton to live, but we didn't move the factory up until a couple of years later. Gail and I flew back and forth from the ranch every day down to the plant. When we finally moved the whole business up to Buellton, it took 13 semi-trailers to transport everything.

When we came up here, we didn't have the print shop we had in Temple City, and we had to buy that out. Also, there wasn't anybody to repair the machines, so we kind of learned how to do that ourselves. And that's the way we've always been. Nobody was there to tell us we couldn't do something, so we did it.

We eventually bought a small printing press, because it was taking too long for the local guys to print our stuff. I thought I knew a lot about printing because I'd watched my dad when I was young. Then Tony and I took some graphics and printing classes up at Allan Hancock College in nearby Santa Maria, which added to our abilities in the printing area.

We had a card-carrying industrial engineer who planned the move from Temple City up to Buellton. He planned what product was going to go where. When he came up to Buellton, he marked the floor where the machines were going to be right to the square inch. And he planned where all the electrical was going to be placed.

In the meantime, before we started the move, we'd bought another company called O'Laughlin Manufacturing, a tin company that was located in Temecula. It was owned by an older guy who wanted to retire. He made candle molds for a company that we were manufacturing plastic candle molds for. We were handling the packaging of their wax, scents, wicking and other items. That was one of our custom packaging jobs. That's apparently how we found out about this guy. We'd never been in the sheet metal business, but Gail had a lot of mechanical experience. I went down there and spent about three weeks learning how to set up punch presses, brakes, and shears. And I also learned how to make candle molds. We moved the equipment up and we made candle molds for a company called Yaley Enterprises in San Francisco. We had a hard time because the learning period was really long.

We got the concept right away, but it took a while to get the hang of making molds that didn't leak. Then we designed our own line of early American tinware. Aleene and Gail flew back to Sturbridge Village, Massachusetts, and bought antiques and reproductions of things that we designed around.

We bought several little companies, including one called LeJeune, a company that imported a synthetic raffia from Switzerland. They also had dyes, which we started packaging. Boy, was that a messy job! It was in your nose, under your fingernails--everywhere. We packaged soda ash, which is another component, and also urea for thickening the dye. When we moved to Buellton we had to build a special room to contain all this mess.

In the early days of working with Aleene's Tacky Glue, we used glass jars and put labels on them by hand. We used a pump to do it back then, but when we moved to Buellton in 1974, we bought a machine which was built in 1948. It was a battleship-type contraption which did two bottles at a time. It had a conveyor that pushed the bottles along and raised them up to fill them. We hired a local couple, Bud and Ida, to work with us. She was probably 65 at the time, and he was 69. They were great workers. Bud and Ida and I filled 100 cases of 72 bottles every day. If the machine broke down, we generally worked until 7 o'clock in the evening instead of 5 o'clock. They lived in a trailer park across the way. He'd retired from 35 years at Union Oil, and she'd been a housewife. They also worked at the local newspaper stuffing inserts into the paper on Thursdays. They worked with us for a long time. Then finally, their health declined so they retired. But they were a beautiful couple, and like so many people

Fred's newest home, a 36 foot Cal-Cruising sailboat named "Chow."

who've been involved with Artis/Aleene's, they had a great spirit that they brought with them to our projects.

Aleene was an un-traditional salesperson, who has always had the knack for opening the right doors leading to a sale. I went with her sometimes, to places like J.C. Penney's in New York, when she was introducing new products. She would get out the little black boxes she carried and lay out all her products on the table. She'd describe how to use it all, and get the buyers all excited. Then, to their surprise, she'd pack it up and leave. She would never actually take an order. That was somebody else's job. She would demonstrate and get them all excited about potential sales, then she wouldn't take the order. In fact, she went to KMart's buyer one time, and told him she wasn't ready to sell to him yet. He said, "Ma'am, you're the first person who ever came in here and pitched me, but refused to take an order." Aleene laughed, and told him that Gail or someone from the plant would be calling to take the order.

If you look back at Aleene's parents, Grandpa and Grandma Jackson, you can see a lot of where Aleene's spirit and abilities come from. Both of them were in the business. Grandpa Jackson, who weighed about 300 pounds, was the nicest man you'd ever want to meet. Grandma weighed just over 80 pounds, so I guess it kind of balanced out.

When Aleene was young, I can just imagine that my grandmother had no control over her at all, absolutely none. She'd just completely run with whatever she wanted to do. And I'm sure she's exactly the same way now as she was when she was a kid-- determined, focused, and still going strong at 72!

Heidi and third husband Harold Borchers.

Heidi Borchers,
Born October 30, 1949

My third child, Heidi, was as sensitive as Fred was tough. When Fred was naughty, there was a time or two that I had to take a strap to him, because nothing fazed him. You could smack him, and he would stand there and defy you. Then along came Heidi, and if you looked at her the wrong way, she'd break out crying, she was that sensitive. When Heidi was two, she had bronchial pneumonia and almost died. She was very private, the kind of child who, if she was having a problem, wouldn't think of discussing it with you. Even recently, I was having a discussion with her about something or other and she started to cry. I hadn't seen that in a long time, but she's one of those people who are really sensitive, in the best sense of the word.

Heidi was always the most artistic of my kids, a natural-born designer. When we had holiday parties, Heidi used to decorate the house in the most unusual and unique ways. She had the good fortune to apprentice with Katie Ogle, my principal designer who later died in the airplane crash, with Gail at the controls. When I lost Katie, I knew that Heidi had enough background to do some of our work. But I was amazed at how quickly she was able to take over Katie's place. Heidi could do anything, quickly and creatively. So much so, that as the years went by, I came to believe that she is probably one of the top five most creative people in our craft industry. She has really new ideas, and is always focused on presenting them so that anyone can do them. Heidi's love is for the fun things, the decorative and quick projects that appeal to large num-

Heidi's children from left to right: Grady, Starr and Woody.

bers of people. When we started coming back with Aleene's Tacky Glue, She was very instrumental in Aleene's. She'd do instructions for projects with the ease of a long-time master of the art, and from early on, too. I remember that she did the instructions for our first Shrink-Art products, and yet she was very young at that time.

At present, Heidi and her husband Harold are completing a beautiful house on the California coast. At the same time she's been designing for our publisher, Oxmoor House, finishing three new crafts books for them. Heidi's oldest son, Woody, 27, (who has devoted much of his time to laying out this book.) currently working in our art department in Buellton. Grady, 26, is working for Doug Cramer Productions in Burbank, helping to develop new television programs. Heidi's daughter, Starr, had been in the medical field, but is now working with Heidi on a number of projects as her assistant.

Always developing a number of things at the same time, Heidi and daughter, Starr, just published their first book, In the writing, art and design, Where Do Angels Buy Their Clothes? I have to say, that it is a beautiful book.

From the desk of Heidi.

We always worked in the store after school and during the summers, packaging leaves and all the many little parts that Alcene sold. From the time we were little kids, she had us in the back packaging things. The family always helped out on everything. That was how we made money to buy clothes and things we wanted. I remember starting at 10¢ an hour, and being raised to 25¢ an hour. As we got older, we just helped wherever necessary.

At Christmas time, orders had to be filled, so I worked in the wholesale division pulling and filling orders. We worked Saturdays and Sundays, whatever it took to get the orders out. Then when I was in high school I worked in the retail store. When we were younger, when Mom had the retail store, she always put us in whatever class was going on. Maybe it was a kind of baby-sitting ser-

Heidi and her second husband George Atiyeh. Pictured with Woody, Grady and Starr.

vice for her, but it ended up being training for us. She
would have us sitting in the class while she went up
front and did the work. It was a little different when
Tony and Tiffany came along. That was the period
when Aurora had taken over Aleene's, Inc. When we
were little, we rang the register in the retail store before
we could even reach it. We had a step stool to stand on,
and Mom taught us how to ring the register and count
out money. You might say it was the original "Camp
Aleene."

Years later, when I had my own kids, if they
were bad or unruly, they got sent to "Camp Aleene,"
where they had to do the same thing--work. Aleene
always made them work and toe the line. And sometimes the kids would beg me, "No, Mom, don't send
me to Camp Aleene!" I have eight grandchildren now
between my husband's and my kids. My kids have four,
and his kids have four, and sometimes they wonder if

Heidi's wedding to Jimmy Gray Hall. Candy, Maid of Honor,
Tiffany, Jr. Bridesmaid and Tony, Ring Bearer

there's gonna be a "Camp Heidi," since Mom's "Camp Aleene" is closed.

But when Candy, Fred and I were little, we did a lot of work and took almost every class that was given. Aleene had flower-making, cake decorating, and Christmas decorations classes, among others. I worked in the store throughout high school, and just before I graduated, I became manager of Mom's retail store. That lasted for a couple of years and only ended, really, when she and Gail sold out to Aurora.

Grandma Jackson ran the mail order department for many years. That was her division. Grandpa had gone over to run Snowfoam, so he was in and out a lot. When the store closed and Aurora bought out Aleene's, Inc., our grandparents kept the mail order part of the business, and I joined them in it. We ended up running the mail order business for 20 years, from 1969 on. Grandpa Jackson sold me the mail order business in 1980, because Grandma had became real ill and he was taking care of her. I then ran it until 1989, when I sold it.

To begin with we only sold Aleene's products. Later we added a few products that were not our own. We started out calling it the "Mail Order Craft Source." Then when we went wholesale, we just called it the "Craft Source." Before we developed our mail order catalog, Mom had created "The Petal Pusher" in the form of little leaflets. She used to do it monthly. Then it turned into a color brochure called, "The Craft Maker." Our very first catalog in the mail order was just a typewritten thing that had the supplies that were in this first little leaflet, I think it was a Valentine's Day project. It was just a one-page flyer that we would send out to all the Aleene's customers on the mail order list.

It was a color leaflet showing how to make some Valentine designs, and had a typewritten list of supplies. That was how we started the mail order. Aleene's, Inc., had had a catalog for years, but at first we didn't have the money to put into one. As the years went by though, we developed a big 60-page catalog. We added supplies, but my main business for the 20 years was selling the Aleene's products, the glues and everything else. We became a wholesale distributor for Aleene's supplies, starting with smaller dealers who needed to break up a case of supplies. Aleene's, Inc., would have the customer call us because we would break a case. If they had a store and wanted six bottles or whatever, we would sell to these smaller dealers. So, as soon as that happened, we became wholesalers and sold to stores, too. From there we began to sell a lot of our floral supplies.

The mail order was in a store. My grandfather

Heidi's wedding to George Atiyeh. Tiffany, Maid of Honor.

owned the building that Aleene's retail store was in, and when Aleene's dissolved and Aurora bought it, my grandfather sold the building. The gentleman he sold it to owned a refrigeration company and allowed us to rent part of it back. For about 12 years we rented a little place, at $250 a month, and he never raised our rent. It was probably 1500 square feet. Then it got so big, with so many supplies, that I moved next door, and had a very large store. Then we decided we didn't want to pay that kind of rent money and so we bought another building.

During the days of the Craft Caravans, I usually worked in the bookstore, keeping it running. I filled in at a lot of different things, working everywhere, demonstrating how-to, or whatever was necessary. I went out on a lot of the shows, but not every single one.

The Craft Caravan was always exciting because there were so many people. It was a giant rush of people coming because of their interest in crafts. And the Crafts Caravan really was the birth of the crafts industry in this country. So many people in so many cities got to see first hand what it was all about. Aleene, along with Hazel Pearson, really helped give birth to the whole thing. When I had the retail store, we did a couple of open houses at Aleene's, and it was at the open houses where the "Make-It-And-Take-It" idea began. We started it at open houses at her store, where people could come in and make something that they didn't have to pay for. That was a way to promote the supplies we were selling. So we would do a lot of open houses during the year. We'd do a Spring, Summer and Fall Open House, and we'd get a mass of people coming through. All day, I'd just ring the register, talking with the people as I worked, getting to know what they liked and what they didn't. Like Fred and Candy, I was very familiar with all aspects of the whole business.

As children, when we lived in the big house on Longden Avenue in Arcadia, Aleene would always have Christmas open houses. Everybody's room was specially decorated for the holidays, and we kids stood in our rooms, like proper little hosts to all the visitors. Aleene and her team of designers and crafters would go all out for Christmas. And they gave away tickets at the store for people to come through the house.

In the summers, Aleene would decorate the house and invite dealers to come through. The dealers, in turn, would go back and know what to order, since they'd had a preview of what was going to be shown at Christmas time. Then at Christmas Aleene would have all sorts of idea sheets with designs that were done from our products and materials. These we'd sell to the dealers. Often they'd come and make some of those samples to take back to their stores.

But Mom always did weird things, too. One time she had a palm tree in the living room as a Christmas tree! She also liked to have different themes. One year she had Christmas trees hanging from the ceiling upside down. Another year, Mom had a Christmas tree cut into two pieces, vertically. She placed one half outside of a glass bay window, and the other half inside, so that it looked like it had grown right up through the glass! That was our "outdoor-indoor tree." It was such a wonderful, weird thing to look at, with lights and decorations both inside and out.

Aleene had a whole group of designers who were always coming up with ideas for her. She didn't create most of the things herself. She just had the imagination.

And told the designers what she wanted. and when I design, that's still what she does with me. Mom will envision something and tell me to try it. That's where I get a lot of my ideas. We just talk back and forth to get ideas. A lot of times she will send me a magazine page she's ripped out that has an idea or a design on it that sparked her imagination. Nine times out of ten my interpretation is usually completely different, but she feeds me the ideas. We work well together that way, and we've always worked well together, in between the normal mother-and-daughter fights and arguments that is.

One of my favorite designers, Katie Ogle, worked with Mom for years and years. She was the top designer, and the one that stayed on with Aleene when the company became Artis/Aleene's, Inc. She died in a plane crash, the one that Gail was in up in San Francisco. Katie died because she didn't know how to swim. Gail thought she had gotten out, but she didn't know how to swim. Mom had a horrible deadline to meet at the time of the crash, and asked me if I thought I could take over the work that Katie had started. I did it, and I thought I did a really good job. So, from then on I did all the designing for Mom. She would buy designs from people who specialized in certain things, or have them write certain books. I had done some designing at that point, but it wasn't a big part of my life until fate stepped in. It was terribly sad because I adored Katie. She had been one of my mentors, and her death was really painful to all of us. Katie had been with Mom since the early days.

She was an incredible designer. She was the one who invented the "burned brown bag." She was the one who tested the glue for its flammability. She was the one who discovered how to make the glue look like metal when it was burned. Katie spent a lot of time trying to figure out how flammable the glue might be. By burning it, she was able to create a texture that looked like metal when it dried. She also came up with a lot of the early concepts for crafts, like the designs using recycled things. She was the one who taught me how to do that; how to take things and look at them and see how to make something out of them. I'm not the type of designer who draws out the ideas first. Usually I can just look at something and know what I want to do with it.

What's happened over the years is that I don't even like to do the instructions on a design anymore. Tiffany, Mom and I did a book back in the '80's called *Super Scrap Crafts*. I did the design and Tiffany did the instructions for it. That's how *The Big Book of Crafts* started too. I did the design, Tiffany did instructions, and Aleene did a lot of the editorial-type things. The editor at *Big Book* got so familiar with my stuff that I could just send her my list of supplies and she was able to write the instructions for what to do.

A lot of designs have gone into *The Big Book of Crafts*. It was originally going to be a two-year project. We had 24 shipments and each one had 20 designs. It also meant that maybe one of those designs was a necklace and two earrings--it wasn't just one necklace and a pair of earrings. So, it was more than 20 designs, and could have been 30 or 40. If I did a shirt, I usually did two versions of it. But there were actually 20 full page plastic cards that the customer would get over the span of two years. I did all the designs. Tiffany did a couple of them because she does more contemporary things than I do. But, I did everything else.

It was October of 1993 that I quit working exclusively for Aleene's, and decided just to freelance. For the last two and a half years all I've been doing is freelancing. I still freelance for Artis/Aleene, but also do a lot of work for other people and companies. But in the last year or so, my projects for Aleene's and Oxmoor House have taken most of my time.

In addition to my freelance work, I've starting a new company called "Simply Angels." I'm just manufacturing different angel products. Our first product came recently, Spiritual Herbals. They're neat little packages of herbs that I designed and my son Woody helped out with the package design. Also, I'm proud to report that my daughter Starr and I have written a children's book called *Where Do Angels Buy Their Clothes?* I'm self-publishing it and it's just off the press now. So, we're working together a lot. And I've got a lot of other projects that I'm going to manufacture.

Another project I'm involved with now is Oxmoor House's new continuity program called, *The Big Book of Holidays.* It's going to be all holiday-related crafts. We do a lot of designs and celebrations for different holidays. And we did that as kids--we really did. Mom taught us that every holiday was special, and she always had us decorating and creating specifically for each holiday. For Easter celebrations, for example, Aleene would invite hundreds of people over, her employees and her friends. We had almost an acre, and she would hide Easter eggs and candies that were packaged. For weeks before Easter we would pack these little candies, then hide them out in trees and things. Every holiday was like that. Mom always made sure it was a big celebration.

Current picture (1997) as editor of Aleene's Creative Living Magazine, and producer and host of the television show "Aleene's Creative Living" on TNN (The Nashville Network).

Tiffany Windsor, November 25, 1955

After Heidi came Tiffany. She was a wonderful baby, and for some reason, when she was little, Tiffany always drew older people to her. She was really the perfect little daughter until she got to be a teenager. Then Tiffany went through a bit of a rough period, and I know it had to do with my divorcing Woody and marrying Gail. Gail was so different from their father. Woody had been very fine, nice, and quiet. And he was followed by Gail who was a domineering and dictatorial type. The kids weren't used to this kind of controlling father, and it was a shock to them. Tiffany, above all, rebelled at this kind of treatment by Gail.

Tiffany has always had a lot of different abilities, in particular, interior decorating. She didn't pick up her clothes too often when she was young, but the minute she got her own apartment, it was spotless. You couldn't get a glass of water without washing the glass and putting it away! Today, I'm proud of the work Tiffany has done managing our magazine, Creative Living, and her work as producer and on-camera personality on our

Tiffany at about a year and a half old.

television show. We don't always agree, as it is within most families, but the love we feel for each other is always there.

From the desk of Tiffany.

Aleene is a woman ahead of her time in many ways. Sometimes it's hard for me to stand back and look at her from an objective viewpoint, because, after all, she is my mother. When I was younger, I just took it for granted that everyone's mom was like her, but of course that wasn't the case. As an adult, I can look back and say, "In 1947, Aleene did what?" Growing up with Aleene, all of the "women's equality" movement was just a natural part of our life.

What women have been going through for decades, in wanting equal rights in all aspects of life, was something we never questioned in our household. We just lived it. In growing up, I never felt as a woman that I had to "fight" for anything. Now I think it's because we grew up believing what Mom believed -- that by using your brains and common sense, you could accomplish whatever you wanted, regardless of your gender.

Tiffany at age 9.

Tiffany in high school.

When I think about Mom, the main thing I can say is that she never took "no" for an answer. Once she decided which way she was going, she always threw everything she had into her business. That sense of determination is something she has passed on to her children, and for me personally, I think it's the greatest gift she could ever give. I don't know if she "taught" me that or not, but when I set my mind to something I can be very stubborn, very determined.

Mom has always been very creative in her own way. As many people know, she was one of the pioneers when there was no "craft" industry. To go back and take a look at that time in the industry, there she was with the Craftmakers Caravans, launching her products and going in hobby model stores at a time when crafts didn't exist in stores. You have to admit she was definitely a pioneer. To have the foresight and determination to go out and do that, to create an industry where there wasn't one, I can't even think of a way to equate that to today's terms.

Mom also launched and ran her business without financing. It's incredible, looking at it from today's business perspective. I believe it wasn't until recent years that the company borrowed for the first time. Mom started from scratch and did it her way.

Another "custom" was that Mom always

believed in employing family. When I was growing up there were always aunts and uncles and grandparents involved in the family business. As children, my brothers, sisters and I had to work too. Whether is was opening and stuffing mail, counting leaves and stamens or running the cash register in the retail store, it seems as if we spent a lot of time working. As a child, I can remember grumbling about having to work while my friends were out playing. But, as an adult, I am so thankful for all of the work experience and ethics I learned as a child. I am thankful that Mom started the tradition of keeping the family together through the business. Even though there can be differences of opinions between family members, I value the opportunity to work with them.

Mom and a local newscaster had been co-hosting the television show for several years when Mom called me, and asked if I was interested in trying some co-hosting on the show. I had appeared on television with Mom when I was in my early teens and I had the opportunity to travel with her to the Tennessee Ernie Ford and Gypsy Rose Lee shows.

After several attempts at working for the family business in my late teens and early 20's, I returned to work full-time with the family business in January 1993. I decided to return to the business because I was looking for a more creative outlet. I had been involved in commercial real estate development and management for ten years and I wanted to return to a more creative environment. The timing seemed right as my siblings and I had matured into talented businesspeople.

I decided to start on a part-time basis, taping on weekends. On the first segment I was to interview Heidi, who was demonstrating a craft called

Scherenschnitte, which involved cutting silhouettes from paper. I recall that we were taping outside, and it was about 20 degrees and I was shivering and shaking from being cold and extremely nervous. When the cameras were rolling, neither Heidi nor I could say Scherenschnitte to save our lives! Because we were shivering, the words kept coming out wrong. I'll let you guess what it must have sounded like! The show's producer was getting upset with us and Heidi ended up crying (I would have too if it hadn't been so cold -- I guess my tears froze up!) and couldn't stop. So, Mom stepped in and demonstrated the project. I interviewed her and the segment came out good enough for her to invite me back to do more!

From there, I started interviewing more guests on the show. When I became more involved on a full-time basis, I took on more of the production responsibilities and eventually became the producer and host.

Today, my main relationship with Mom is centered around our working together. I don't feel we have a traditional mother-daughter relationship because her whole life is her business. Both being strong opinionated women, we disagree about many business matters.

Lately however, we have through the spiritual mentoring of my sister, Candy, become involved and share an interest in expanding our metaphysical and spiritual awareness. While my interests have ranged from crystals to Reiki, an ancient touch bodywork hands-on healing technique, to angel spirit guides, Mom has found an interest in Deepak Chopra's teachings.

Even though we don't always agree, I love and respect her tremendously.

Tony and Linda, married May 25, 1985.

Tony Hershman,
Born September 8, 1960

The kids always thought that I spoiled Tony because he was my last child, the baby. They thought I liked him better, and maybe I did, because Tony was the one I felt was the most like me. He was always thinking about ways of doing things. When I first moved up to Santa Ynez, Tony stayed with my mother and father because it was early May and he was still finishing school. But as soon as he was out, he moved up with Gail and me, and right away he got into horseback riding. There was a small stable just down the street, and he got to where he loved horses, just like I did. I always

felt like it was fun being around Tony because he was always gung-ho to try something new, or do something that wasn't being done.

I've always felt that Tony was the most like me in spirit, in his ability to keep going when the going gets rough. Even as a child, he had that ability. When we went to enroll him in high school, people thought we were in the wrong school, seeing as how he was so short. They thought surely he isn't old

Tony at about age 4, on a
trip to Hawaii.

enough to be starting high school. Two or three weeks later, though, he was voted freshman class president. The next year, as I remember, he set up a Junior Rodeo at Alisal Ranch, a beautiful and prestigious location. He made all the arrangements, and had no qualms about raising the money. He did everything it took to organize the event. Two or three classmates helped him, but by and large, Tony did it all, and he still does!

Tony and "Joe" 1976.

Tony's high school senior photo.

From the desk of Tony.

If I was introducing Aleene to a gathering of people who didn't know who she was, I'd probably introduce her as the "Mother of all Crafts," one of the original people who helped start the industry and created the foundation of the crafts field that we know today. Aleene was one of the four or five key people who really took the crafts business from nothing, from an idea, really, and helped it blossom into what it is now. And she is certainly the one with the longest track record in it, as well. Of the original five, I don't think any of them are in the business anymore. They're all retired. Mom has continued to follow it through, and that's one of the reasons why our brand name dominates the industry today. It's because of 50 years of her hard work.

Aleene's talents probably lie in her ability to ignore the rest of the industry and do what she feels strongly about. For example, the rest of the industry never advertised to consumers in the past, and as a rule they still don't. They're just starting, maybe in the last year, to look at consumer-based advertising as an important part of their advertising. Aleene, on the other

Tony and mom, at Christmas 1995.

hand, has always gone directly to the consumer in one way or another. Because of her, we've always taken a different approach to selling. If we sell it directly to the consumer, they're going to go into a store and ask for it, and the store is going to go find out how to buy it. We don't go to the store and try to sell to them. We sell it to the consumer, and it's already pre-determined that the store is going to buy it.

As far as my childhood goes, I remember a lot about the business, doing things around our company. I remember going to the Craftmaker's Caravan and announcing the drawings and stuff when I was just five years old. I remember teaching Bread Dough Flowers and having to stand on an 8-foot table because I was so small. I remember getting up on the table in order to be able to see the ladies, and for them to be able to see me, because I couldn't lean over their shoulders and teach them.

I remember working after school at the store in Temple City in the early days of Aleene's, and at our manufacturing operations. Aleene traveled a lot when we were kids, and so we had Audrey, our nanny/house-keeper, who was really like our second mother.

Gail became my stepfather when I was five years old, so he was the primary adult male in my life, and was responsible for a lot of who I am. I have a lot more of Gail's characteristics than I do of my dad's. He was certainly the main cultural influence in my life, for good or bad. At the time, I certainly thought it was very bad. Gail and I didn't get along real well most of the time. But looking back on it, I can see he tried real hard, and what he was doing he thought was the best. And some of it was. The experience and the education that Gail gave me, nobody else in the family could have given me.

My father couldn't have done it. Gail certainly gave me my mechanical background. I wouldn't have been mechanical at all without Gail. And I think that helped me a lot in growing up in the company. I ran the production department out here, in Buellton for a long time. Gail was always there when I needed the help and advice, and often gave it to me whether I wanted it or not.

As far as my working with Artis/Aleene's, Inc., it isn't what I thought I was going to end up doing. In 1978 I went to auctioneering school and became an auctioneer. I took time out from auctioneering to help Mom for two weeks in 1979, and now I've been doing it all of my adult life so far. At about eighteen-and-a-half, I started work on the shipping dock. Over the years, I've ended up doing just about every job there is here, and probably a few no one ever thought about.

If you've read this far in the book, you know about our battle over the bankruptcy. Technically, we're out of bankruptcy now, but still under the jurisdiction of the bankruptcy court. Until all the payments are made, we aren't out of their jurisdiction. If we default we'd be back in front of the judge arguing why we didn't make those payments and why we should get extensions, but we certainly don't anticipate that happening. We anticipate that we'll make the payments on time and be out of the court's jurisdiction. So while we're technically out of bankruptcy, we're still in it. The term that we use, in layman's terms, is that we're out of bankruptcy as of July 14th 1995, because we don't have to go back in front of the judge. But it's kind of like making a loan. You're not in default until you stop making payments.

We filed for bankruptcy in November '93. We

recognized several months before that we had serious problems, and we hired an outside business consultant. Up until that time we made all kinds of jokes about outside business consultants and how worthless they are, but it turned out to be very beneficial for us. Unfortunately, it was too late. We couldn't maneuver enough to avoid the bankruptcy filing, although we tried hard.

There were so many difficult aspects to our business problems, that I don't know where to start. For me personally, it was the most painful, agonizing, torturous challenge, minute after minute, hour after hour. Just when you thought you couldn't get any lower, you got lower. Unfortunately, you drag your family through it with you, and my wife was very supportive.

The attorney told us to begin with that when you go through bankruptcy there are going to be real highs and real lows, and there certainly were. When a company goes into bankruptcy, the first thing people do is want the company to change the management that drove them into bankruptcy, in this case, me. In hindsight, it's a real easy, knee-jerk reaction for creditors to take. You know, let's get rid of these managers who've trashed the company. But after having gone through it, having learned what we did to create problems for the company, and how to keep them from happening again, I can see the benefits of keeping existing management in place.

For one thing, we've been through it. One of Gail's pieces of advice was, don't fire somebody just because they did something wrong. If you can correct it, you can be pretty sure they're not going to do it again - even if it's stealing from you. The creditors wanted me out of the company, but I fought and fought. That was probably my hardest personal battle. Number one, it was my fault the company went into bankruptcy. I knew it, and that was a heavy burden right there. I know now it was my lack of experience in running a business. When I came to work here in '79, our first year we grossed $400,000 in sales. The year we filed bankruptcy we probably did $12 or 13 million. I had no formal business experience. I went to Santa Ynez High, and I didn't know what it took to run a company of the size we were when I took over. So in a lot of ways, I got my MBA in the school of bankruptcy. I felt like I should have gotten the judge to sign off on a graduation certificate by the time it was done. I learned all kinds of things from our business consultant, and from the attorneys, and from being beat up through the process. It was grueling, but I have to thank Aleene for her support, and for standing behind me when everyone was telling her she shouldn't. And thanks to my wife Linda, for supporting me and always being there when I needed it most.

One of the favorite sayings of our business consultant, a kind of stuffy Harvard man, was "what doesn't kill me makes me stronger. He loved to quote all the ancient philosophers and their wonderful little sayings. I developed a real love/hate relationship with him. I knew he was like a doctor, come to help heal our business, but we kept arguing about the cures. I think that was part of the process in learning how to evaluate things on a higher level than we'd ever evaluated them before. Before we went into bankruptcy we didn't have a good management plan or systems in the company. Kind of like, "Yeah, that product looks good, let's do it." We never planned how much money it would take; what the investment was, what's the expected return

was; how many pieces do we expect to sell; and what's
the risk? We never even assessed it. It was just a gut-
level reaction, like this sounds good, let's do it! Now we
don't do that. We go through a very detailed analysis of
any program we're considering. Even when we're re-
evaluating our already existing programs we continue
to go through a detailed business analysis. Is it on track,
is it doing what it's supposed to be doing, is it doing
what we projected it would do when we envisioned it?
Is it above or below? If it's below, what does it need to
get back on track? If it's above, what did we do right
that we can apply to other programs we're doing? That
kind of detailed look at our business practices was
something we never did before.

Bankruptcy was the most painful thing you can
ever imagine. There's no way to write about it. They
told us going into it: Do anything to avoid bankruptcy.
Sell the company, give the company away, walk away,
throw up your hands - do anything. Even our own
bankruptcy attorney said it. We considered all our
options, and finally just got mad and said we were
going to take the bull by the horns and make our way
through it. It was just plain tenacity that did it.

There were days when I was down and Aleene
would have to pull me through it, and days she was
down I'd have to pull her through it, days we were both
down and our associates pulled us through it. And my
wife Linda was always there to pick me up when I needed it most. There were many times when I wanted to
throw in the towel, but I couldn't do it because of the
100 associates and their families who make their living
at Artis/Aleene's, Inc. Many of our people have put in a
lot of years here, and a number of them started with us
right out of high school. When you have people who

have been here thirteen, fourteen, or even fifteen years, and they're only in their mid-30s, they've spent their whole adult lives with the company, so you feel like you've got to do whatever it takes to keep it going.

Aleene's employees really got behind our effort to save the company through the bankruptcy. In the first months of the bankruptcy, 80-hour weeks weren't uncommon for the associates. There were times we would work all day long, all night long until four in the morning, get two hours sleep, and then hit it again.

It's something you can't walk away from, can't get out of. Things keep hitting you from every direction. People you expect to react in certain ways--certain creditors where you expected to get no reaction or a supportive reaction, you would get a negative reaction. And creditors you expected to be negative were very supportive. Ultimately, it was Aleene's customers who saved us. Without what the customers did for us, we wouldn't have made it. We had customers who knew we were in difficulties, and they turned around and advanced us money against orders that they'd already placed. Aleene raised half a million dollars in three days, against advances on open orders. For a company in Chapter 11 to get advances from their customers is totally unheard of. None of the professionals in our case, including the judge, could believe it. Where one week earlier we had no money, suddenly we had half a million dollars and were jump-started again. There was only one company that said no, out of the thirty-nine customers we called to help us with advance payments on their orders, and I think that says a lot about their feelings both for Mom, and for Artis/Aleene's, as a whole.

The crafts industry is an evolving one, so it isn't

easy to say where it's headed. The business has evolved so much in the last ten years, that where it will be five or ten years from now is anybody's guess.

I think that over the last decade the independent craft store has become extinct. I think they'll come back again and find a niche for themselves. Soon they'll compete against the big chains that have come in, like WalMarts and Michaels stores, and the big fabric stores, too. I think the industry is going to continue growing. As time progresses, the crafts industry will focus more on the end customer, and on consumer advertising, which they haven't done in the last ten years.

The prevailing philosophy of our industry right now is that the manufacturer should do 90% of the work, letting the consumer finish it, but also letting the consumer take 100% of the credit for the project. The manufacturer does the work - you don't necessarily have to be a crafter or have talent to do crafts anymore. The projects are so simplified that literally anybody can do them. And that also makes this a more feasible industry to a much broader segment of the demographics. Overall, I think this makes the future bright, both for Artis/Aleene's, Inc., and our industry as a whole.

Tony & Linda circa 1985.
Tony's horse "Joe". (born 1974 - died 1996)
Linda's horse "Shoana". (born 1982)

From left to right, my grandfather Jackson, my father, my grandmother and my aunt Lois. My father was around age 18 at this time.

Lois Florence Net Ann Vera Grandpa 1926 Dad

A family picture from 1926. Aleene at age 2.

Dr. Offerman, my grandfather, on my mothers side.

Great Grandma Jackson, Great Grandma Vandever and Candy at
around age 1-1/2.

This picture was me "kidding around" on a horseback ride from Los Angeles to Santa Barbara.

Both of these pictures were taken before I was married. One, a glamour photo, and the other, a business portrait.

Hazel Pearson.
If I was the "Mother of crafts," Hazel was the "Grandmother of crafts."
This picture shows Hazel involved in copper tooling, taken at about the
time that I first met Hazel.

Papa Jackson when he headed Aleene's Fibre and Floral Supply Co. in
the late 1950's. This was before we separated SnowFoam® from
Aleene's, and he moved to the Styrofoam® plant, leaving me with
Aleene's.

Family outing to the Santa Barbara Fiesta. We camped out at the beach.

Audrey and Paul Moore.
Audrey was our housekeeper and housemother for 17 years.

Aleene and Woody in 1953.

Aleene and Gordon Baker Lloyd in 1952-53.

Pictured are pioneers in the Hobby Association. The gentleman behind me was the one whom Hazel and I persuaded to start the Profitable Craft Merchandising Magazine (PCM).

I am very proud that I was chosen "Mother of the Year" by the Los Angeles Examiner newspaper.

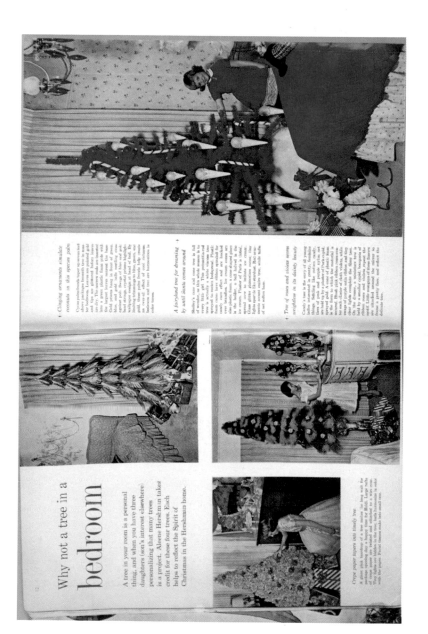

Why not a tree in a bedroom

A tree in your room is a personal thing, and when you have three daughters (son's interest elsewhere) personalizing that many trees is a project. Aleene Hershman takes credit for these four trees. Each helps to reflect the Spirit of Christmas in the Hershman home.

▸ Clinging ornaments simulate coconuts on this species palm

▸ A fairyland tree for dreaming by until sleep comes around

▸ Tree of roses and violets seems neighbors in its dainty beauty

▸ Crisp paper tapers into timely tree

Every now and again I decorated an upside down
Christmas tree, just for the fun of it.

We first taped at our ranch, Tialto. When I sold the ranch, we taped at
friends' houses until we built our own TV studio.

This is the kitchen setting in our new television studio in Buellton, California.

This is the living room setting in our new television studio in Buellton, California.

I don't know when this picture was taken, but I wish I still
looked like that!

My mare "Whoopie Maid"

Heidi, with one of her famous tea parties. Me, with the dark glasses on, at the time of my face lift.

I rented a place at the beach to see if I liked it. Decided to stay in Santa Ynez Valley.

If you visited a craft store or craft department of your favorite store, this is the display you would find.

A Christmas gathering 1994.